English
FOR COMMON ENTRANCE
13+
Exam Practice Questions

Amanda Alexander and Rachel Gee
Subject Editor: Kornel Kossuth

AN HACHETTE UK COMPANY

About the authors

Amanda Alexander and Rachel Gee have extensive experience in teaching and managing in both state and private schools. They have a wealth of knowledge and considerable expertise in preparing children for English at 13+, which they bring to this book. They were the authors of the first edition of *English Practice Exercises 13+*.

Acknowledgements

The Publishers would like to thank Kornel Kossuth for all his support in producing this book.

The Publishers would like to thank the following for permission to reproduce copyright material.

Acknowledgements: **p 2** Asne Seierstad: from *The Bookseller of Kabul* (Hachette Book Group), permission sought; **p 6** Kate Grenville: from *The Idea of Perfection* (Macmillan), permission sought; **p 8** David Nicholls: from 'Every Good Boy' (Guardian, 22 June 2011); **p 12** Sebastian Coe: from *The Winning Mind* (Peters, Fraser & Dunlop), permission sought; **p 16** John Steinbeck: from *Travels with Charley* (US rights The Curtis Publishing Co., UK rights Penguin Random House Ltd.), permission sought; **p 20** Michael Palin: from *Brazil* (The Orion Publishing Group), permission sought; **p 24** Rudyard Kipling: from 'The Finest Story in the World' (United Agents); **p 28** Jack London: from *White Fang*; **p 32** Charles Dickens: from *Great Expectations*; **p 36** Alan Bennett: from *The History Boys* (Faber & Faber Ltd.), permission sought; **p 40** Phoebe Hesketh: from 'Paint Box' (Enitharmon Press); **p 42** Ted Hughes: from 'Fox' (Faber & Faber Ltd.), permission sought; **p 44** Tom Earley: from 'Frustration'; **p 46** John Agard: from 'Flag' (Blood Axe Books); **p 48** James Kirkup: from 'The Caged Bird in Springtime' (Faber & Faber Ltd.); **p 50** Robert Frost: from 'Going for Water'; **p 52** W.H. Davies: from 'The Hermit'; **p 54** Norman MacCaig: from 'Sleet' (Polygon), permission sought; **p 56** Samuel Taylor Coleridge: from 'The Rime of the Ancient Mariner'; **p 58** Thomas Hood: from 'Silence' (Penguin Random House).

Orders: please contact Bookpoint Ltd, 130 Park Drive, Milton Park, Abingdon, Oxon OX14 4SE.
Telephone: (44) 01235 827720. Fax: (44) 01235 400454. Email education@bookpoint.co.uk Lines are open from 9 a.m. to 5 p.m., Monday to Saturday, with a 24-hour message answering service. Visit our website at www.galorepark.co.uk for details of other revision guides for Common Entrance, examination papers and Galore Park publications.

ISBN: 978 1 4718 6896 2

First published in 2016 by

Galore Park Publishing Ltd,
An Hachette UK Company

Carmelite House
50 Victoria Embankment
London EC4Y 0DZ

www.galorepark.co.uk

Impression number 10 9 8 7 6 5 4 3 2 1
Year 2020 2019 2018 2017 2016

Typeset in India

Printed in the UK

A catalogue record for this title is available from the British Library.

Contents

Introduction

As described in the syllabus on pages vi–vii candidates are required to respond to reading and writing tasks across two papers.

This book contains reading and writing practice exercises for both Level 1 and Level 2 candidates. Candidates should ensure that they practise the level recommended by their school. Level 1 and Level 2 candidates share the same extracts and poems but the Level 1 texts may be abridged. Questions are of an appropriate standard according to the reading skills required for each level (see page viii for the Level 1 requirements).

Pages 2–39 provide practice in literary prose comprehensions. Pages 40–59 provide practice in unseen poetry comprehension.

The comprehension exercises are followed by writing tasks, which are the same for both levels. Pages 61–65 provide titles for writing for practical purposes and on literary topics. Pages 67–70 provide titles for writing creatively, provoking imaginative, descriptive and narrative responses.

The accompanying answer book provides additional advice for the teacher and parent but also enables candidates to understand the final expectation and so monitor their progress.

ISEB Common Entrance Examination at 13+ English Syllabus

Candidates will be required to take two papers, both comprising a reading section and a writing section. The reading sections will be divided into two levels: Level 1 and Level 2. The passage and the poem will be the same for both levels, although the passage will sometimes be abridged for Level 1. For both the prose and poetry sections, questions will be easier on the Level 1 paper. The writing sections are common to both Level 1 and Level 2 candidates.

Paper 1 (50 marks; 1 hour 15 minutes, which includes reading and note-making time). The paper will be divided into two sections:

- **Section A: Reading** (25 marks)
- This section will contain a passage of literary prose followed by about five questions which seek to test understanding as well as powers of analysis and evaluation.
- **Section B: Writing** (25 marks)
- Candidates will be asked to select one of four essay titles. Three essay titles will require the use of prose for a practical purpose; the fourth essay title will be a choice of literary topics. Candidates' planning sheets will not be sent to the senior school.

Paper 2 (50 marks; 1 hour 15 minutes, which includes planning time)
The paper will be divided into two sections:

- **Section A: Reading** (25 marks)
- This section will comprise about five questions on an unseen poem to test both understanding of poetic technique and personal response.
- **Section B: Writing** (25 marks)
- Candidates will be asked to choose one of four essay titles which provoke imaginative, descriptive or narrative responses. Candidates' planning sheets will not be sent to the senior school.

Paper 1 Section A: Literary prose

Candidates are given a passage of literary prose from a novel, a play, a biography or travel writing. This is followed by questions to test understanding as well as powers of analysis and evaluation. Passages are selected at the setters' discretion without any standard pattern, in order to encourage a variety of approaches to the reading of quality fiction. An introductory line of explanation may precede the extracts. Certain words may be glossed.

Skills to be tested at the appropriate level include:

- basic understanding and vocabulary
- use of text to illustrate answers
- drawing of inferences
- evaluation of style, language and purpose
- delivery of opinions/judgements/arguments based on given material
- awareness of how grammar, syntax and punctuation affect meaning
- capacity to make comparisons and evaluate contrasts.

Candidates are encouraged to read widely, to acquire and develop the skills of discriminating reading and to express their responses to what they read.

Paper 2 Section A: Poetry

Candidates are given one piece of unseen poetry which may be an entire poem or an extract. This is followed by questions – a literary comprehension, in effect. Candidates are expected to show awareness of how language is used and to support opinion by reference to the text. Questions ask for candidates' responses to literature via an understanding of how writers achieve their effects, reveal their feelings and make readers more aware. This assumes knowledge of metaphor, simile, personification, symbol, irony, alliteration, assonance, rhyme, rhythm and metre.

Papers 1 and 2 Section B: Writing

Response to writing task

Candidates are required to answer two questions from a range of options. Some options require the use of prose for a practical purpose: to argue, persuade, explain, advise, inform. Other options provoke imaginative, descriptive or narrative responses. In addition, there is the option to write on one or more texts which candidates have studied in class or read for themselves. Questions are general and not related to any specific text. They offer candidates the opportunity to deal with moments of drama, transition, contrast and various other ideas in their chosen texts. Texts studied should range across genre and period. Candidates should be encouraged and helped to discuss their reading and analyse their ideas closely.

ISEB Level 1 reading skills

Basic understanding and vocabulary

Candidates will not be expected to explain difficult words.

Use of text to illustrate answers

Candidates will be directed to specific sections of the passage rather than expected to scan the whole text.

Drawing of inferences

Candidates will be expected to recognise feelings/tones/moods by finding examples but will not be expected to infer the mood for themselves. If the writer is angry, this will be stated in the question and candidates will be expected to support this view.

Evaluation of style/language/purpose

Grammar/syntax/punctuation

Capacity to make comparisons and evaluate contrasts

Candidates may be encouraged to think about such features of the text. Questions, however, will identify the use of these features in a specified section of the passage and ask candidates to find examples, explaining briefly why they chose their examples. Alternatively, examples will be identified and candidates may be asked to think about why the writer may have chosen those particular words. If candidates are expected to evaluate contrasts, questions will be structured so as to lead the candidate through the process, e.g. choosing an example, then choosing a contrasting example, then commenting on the difference.

Delivery of opinions/judgements/arguments based on given material

Candidates may be encouraged to give their views on themes and ideas dealt with in the passage but, while reflecting a general understanding of the main concerns of the passage, answers will focus on the candidates' own ideas/experiences.

Knowledge of poetic techniques

Candidates may have to identify examples of simile, metaphor and personification. Questions may identify an example and ask what the technique is, or may explain a technique and ask candidates to find an example. Similarly, they may be asked about onomatopoeia, rhyme and rhythm. They may also have to comment on why a poet might have chosen to use the technique. Candidates will not have to comment on the effectiveness of language in general and will not have to comment on a number of techniques which they have noticed independently.

General guidance for the candidate

The ISEB papers state that:

'Vocabulary, spelling, grammar, punctuation and presentation are important and will be taken into account.'

Vocabulary

Vocabulary choices should be appropriate to the task, sophisticated and engaging. Good vocabulary is impressive.

Spelling

Accuracy is expected but not at the expense of using interesting vocabulary. The spelling of high frequency words and homophones should be sound.

Grammar

Sentences should be accurate with correct grammatical structures in place.

Punctuation

Capital letters should be clearly defined and correctly used. A range of punctuation should be evident and used accurately and clearly to define meaning. Best candidates will use commas, semicolons, colons, dashes, brackets and apostrophes with confidence. Dialogue, where used, should be punctuated and laid out accurately.

Presentation

Handwriting should be consistently well formed in a clear style with regular sizing and spacing. Care should be taken with the demarcation of paragraphs. Crossing out should be limited and neat.

Paper 1 Section A: Reading – Literary prose

Introduction

The texts and questions are all designed to respond to the requirements of the current syllabus (which was first examined in Autumn 2013). In this literary prose section of the book, the passages and questions are designed to test understanding as well as powers of analysis and evaluation across the examined genres. As there is no standard pattern in the setting of literary prose texts at Common Entrance at 13+, a variety of texts has been chosen.

The first two passages are of the same length for both Level 1 and Level 2 candidates. In the subsequent eight passages the Level 1 texts are abridged.

The number and style of questions and the weighting of marks, for Level 1 and Level 2, reflect those of the ISEB exams. The questions are designed to test comprehension skills such as retrieval, the drawing of inferences, deduction and the ability to summarise. In addition, a thorough appreciation of the author's purpose and craft, which assumes knowledge of writing techniques, will enable a personal response that reflects understanding.

The texts, which may be preceded by an introduction, will need a careful and thoughtful reading and candidates should be encouraged to practise immersing themselves in the text at this important stage. It is advisable to read all the questions thoroughly, focusing on the key words. The allocation of marks should be carefully noted and used as a guide to understand the number of points needed and the level of detail required. It may be necessary to think briefly through the structure of an answer, and to find supporting quotations, before starting to write. Responses should directly answer the question and be expressed clearly. The best supporting evidence or examples should be selected and candidates should sufficiently explain their point. Within an answer, candidates may be asked for their personal response and should be encouraged to form opinions based on what they have read. Care should be taken with the spelling of subject-specific words and difficult vocabulary in the text. Careful vocabulary choices, punctuation and presentation all help to create a strong impression.

The allowed time for the complete Paper 1 is 1 hour and 15 minutes. If these exercises are to be completed under exam conditions, approximately 35 minutes should be allowed. It is advisable to leave time to check at the end. However, the texts could also be used to practise key comprehension skills without the time pressure.

The accompanying answer book provides additional advice for the teacher and parent but also enables candidates to understand the final expectation and so monitor their progress.

Level 1

1 *The Bookseller of Kabul* by Asne Seierstad

In this extract, Mansur and his friends are making a journey from Kabul, in Afghanistan, to a New Year Festival some miles away.

Mansur spends the night with Akbar to make sure he wakes up. The next morning, before dawn, they are off. Mansur's only luggage consists of a plastic bag full of Coke and Fanta cans and biscuits with banana and kiwi filling. Akbar has a friend with him and everyone is in high spirits. They play Indian film music
5 and sing at the top of their voices. Mansur has brought his treasure with him, a western cassette, *Pop from the 80s*. 'Is this love? Baby, don't hurt me, don't hurt me no more' resounds out into the cool morning. Before they have driven half an hour Mansur has eaten the first packet of biscuits and drunk two Cokes. He feels free. He wants to scream and shout, and sticks his head out of the window.
10 'Ouhhhhiiii! Here I come!'

They pass areas he has never before seen. Immediately north of Kabul is the Shomali Plain – one of the most war-torn areas of Afghanistan. Here bombs from American B52s shook the ground only a few months ago. 'How beautiful,' Mansur shouts. And from a distance the plain is beautiful, against the backdrop of the
15 mighty snow-clad Hindu Kush mountains that proudly rise up to the sky.

Mansur stares in silence at the awful villages they pass. Most of them are in ruins and rear up in the landscape like skeletons. The remains of twisted tanks, wrecked military vehicles and bits of metal, whose purpose Mansur can only guess at, lie thrown around. A lonely man walks behind a plough. In the middle of his patch
20 lies a large tank. He walks laboriously around it – it is too heavy to move.

The car drives fast over the potholed road. Mansur tries to spot his mother's village. He has not been there since he was five or six. His finger constantly points to more ruins. 'There! There!' But nothing distinguishes one village from another. The place where he visited his mother's relatives as a little boy could be any one of
25 these heaps of rubble. He remembers how he ran around on the paths and fields. Now the plain is the most mined place in the world. Only the roads are safe. Children with bundles of firewood and women with buckets of water walk along the side of the road. They try to avoid the ditches where the mines might be. The ditches are full of wild, dark-red short-stemmed tulips. But the flowers must be
30 admired at a distance. Picking them would be risky.

Akbar is having fun with a book published by the Afghan Tourist Organisation in 1967. 'Along the roads children sell chains of pink tulips', he reads. 'In the spring cherries, apricots, almond and pear trees jostle for the attention of the traveller. A flowering spectacle follows the traveller all the way to Kabul.' They laugh. This
35 spring they spot a lone rebellious cherry tree or two that have survived bombs, rockets, a three-year drought and poisoned wells.

Level 1

1 Look at lines 1–10.

Everyone is in 'high spirits'. (line 4)

a) Find and write down two phrases from the first paragraph that show this. (2)

b) Why do you think they are in such 'high spirits'? (2)

2 Look at lines 13–17.

a) '"How beautiful," Mansur shouts.' (line 13)
What strikes Mansur as beautiful? Explain in your own words. (2)

b) He then 'stares in silence' (line 16). Identify the simile used to describe the war-torn scene he is staring at. (1)
Describe the picture this simile creates in your mind. (2)

3 Look at lines 21–30.

Write down three short quotations which show how the area has changed since Mansur was there as a younger boy and explain how these changes affect the local people. (6)

4 Look at lines 31–36.

a) Akbar and Mansur 'laugh' (line 34) at the tourist book they are reading. Explain why they are laughing. (3)

b) There is one sign of nature that has defied the war: 'they spot a lone rebellious cherry tree or two that have survived bombs ...' (line 35)
Name the writing technique the author has used here and explain why it is effective. (1 + 2)

5 How do you react to the behaviour of the boys as they travel through the area noticing everything around them? (4)

Total: 25

Level 2

1 *The Bookseller of Kabul* by Asne Seierstad

In this extract, Mansur and his friends are making a journey from Kabul, in Afghanistan, to a New Year Festival some miles away.

Mansur spends the night with Akbar to make sure he wakes up. The next morning, before dawn, they are off. Mansur's only luggage consists of a plastic bag full of Coke and Fanta cans and biscuits with banana and kiwi filling. Akbar has a friend with him and everyone is in high spirits. They play Indian film music
5 and sing at the top of their voices. Mansur has brought his treasure with him, a western cassette, *Pop from the 80s*. 'Is this love? Baby, don't hurt me, don't hurt me no more' resounds out into the cool morning. Before they have driven half an hour Mansur has eaten the first packet of biscuits and drunk two Cokes. He feels free. He wants to scream and shout, and sticks his head out of the window.
10 'Ouhhhhiiii! Here I come!'

They pass areas he has never before seen. Immediately north of Kabul is the Shomali Plain – one of the most war-torn areas of Afghanistan. Here bombs from American B52s shook the ground only a few months ago. 'How beautiful,' Mansur shouts. And from a distance the plain is beautiful, against the backdrop of the
15 mighty snow-clad Hindu Kush mountains that proudly rise up to the sky.

Mansur stares in silence at the awful villages they pass. Most of them are in ruins and rear up in the landscape like skeletons. The remains of twisted tanks, wrecked military vehicles and bits of metal, whose purpose Mansur can only guess at, lie thrown around. A lonely man walks behind a plough. In the middle of his patch
20 lies a large tank. He walks laboriously around it – it is too heavy to move.

The car drives fast over the potholed road. Mansur tries to spot his mother's village. He has not been there since he was five or six. His finger constantly points to more ruins. 'There! There!' But nothing distinguishes one village from another. The place where he visited his mother's relatives as a little boy could be any one
25 of these heaps of rubble. He remembers how he ran around on the paths and fields. Now the plain is the most mined place in the world. Only the roads are safe. Children with bundles of firewood and women with buckets of water walk along the side of the road. They try to avoid the ditches where the mines might be. The ditches are full of wild, dark-red short-stemmed tulips. But the flowers must be
30 admired at a distance. Picking them would be risky.

Akbar is having fun with a book published by the Afghan Tourist Organisation in 1967. 'Along the roads children sell chains of pink tulips', he reads. 'In the spring cherries, apricots, almond and pear trees jostle for the attention of the traveller. A flowering spectacle follows the traveller all the way to Kabul.' They laugh. This
35 spring they spot a lone rebellious cherry tree or two that have survived bombs, rockets, a three-year drought and poisoned wells.

Level 2

1 Look at lines 1–10.

Everyone is in 'high spirits' in paragraph one.

How does the author enable us to sense the feeling of excitement? In your answer you should refer to:

- the boys' behaviour
- the effect of the use of tense. (4)

2 Look at lines 21–26.

How does the writer create a vivid picture of the Hindu Kush mountains and the villages?

Each time explain the effect. (6)

3 The boys and the villagers have very different lives. In your own words explain these differences. (5)

4 Look at lines 21–26.

What are Mansur's feelings as he observes the ruined area where his mother lived? (4)

5 Look at lines 28–36.

Flowers and trees seem to be symbolic. Explain three of these symbols. (6)

Total: 25

Levels 1 & 2

2 *The Idea of Perfection* by Kate Grenville

Harley has arrived from the city to spend some time working in Kara Karook, a small township in New South Wales, Australia. The lady she will be working with is called Coralie and she has been loaned the house of Lorraine Smart (who is away on family business) for her stay.

Coralie had been right that Lorraine Smart's house was *not real flash*. The front gate sagged off a single hinge and a length of gutter slanted across the front porch like a demonstration of something in geometry. Inside everything was broken, faded, worn-out, improvised: the kitchen window with a length of white cord
5 hanging out of its sash like a rude tongue, the mantelpiece full of glass swans and china horses that had been broken and glued together again, the laundry where the taps were covered by a brown-paper bag with DO NOT USE in big letters.

Harley had dreaded Lorraine Smart's house, imagining matching tea-cups that she would chip, and polished tables that she would scratch, and a Master Bedroom
10 with the private shape of someone else's feet still in the shoes in the wardrobe, and the troughs made by other people's lives still in the mattress.

But she was starting to feel that she would probably like Lorraine Smart, whoever she was. She liked the fact that the ornaments had all been broken at least once already, and when the kitchen tap came off in her hand and had to be fitted back
15 on, she felt at home. The fridge door, speckled with dust, as if it had measles, was covered with photos of people lined up, squinting at the camera, smiling. In some of them you could see the shadow of the photographer, stretching out over the grass to meet them.

A space had been cleared among the photos for a note: *Welcome, make yourself*
20 *at home. Best regards, Lorraine* held on with a pineapple-shaped magnet that said *Greetings from Rockhampton.*

The kitchen window looked out over the backyard, which was not real flash either. There was grass as faded and dry as straw from the drought, and a few limp shrubs, and dead sticks where other shrubs had given up. There was a big messy
25 gum tree hung with ragged ribbons of bark, and underneath it, tilting on the hard ground, a Garden Setting[1] in white plastic. There was a Hills Hoist[2] with a little brick path leading out to it, and a square of pink concrete underneath to stand on while you pegged out the washing. A bare wire archway with a few dead sticks tangled in it had obviously been meant to have roses rambling over it.

30 Harley opened the window and leaned out. The sun was beginning to lower itself down toward the hills and although it was still hot the light was beginning to thicken into gold.

It was another planet out here. The city became merely a dream, or as distant as something you had read about in a book: something you could remember, or not,
35 as you pleased. The country made the city and all its anxieties seem small and silly, and yet when you had been too long in the city, you forgot how the sun moving through its path was a long slow drama, and the way the sky was always there, big and easy-going.

1 Garden tables and chairs
2 Rotary clothes line

Level 1

1 Look at lines 1–7.

Lorraine Smart's house was '*not real flash*'. (line 1)

a) Explain what you think this means. (1)

b) Write down two quotations from paragraph one which suggest this, one describing the outside of the house and one describing the inside of the house. (2)

2 Look at lines 8–11.

Explain why Harley 'had dreaded' staying in Lorraine Smart's house. Give three reasons, supported by quotations. (6)

3 Look at lines 13–21.

Using quotations, explain two different impressions you have of Lorraine Smart. (6)

4 a) Name the two forms of imagery quoted below:

'There was grass as faded and dry as straw' (line 23)

'ribbons of bark' (line 25) (2)

b) Explain both images. (4)

5 Look at lines 30–38.

When Harley opens the window she thinks it is 'another planet out here' (line 33). Give two reasons, with evidence, why she thinks this. (4)

Total: 25

Level 2

1 Look at lines 1–7.

What are Harley's first impressions, from paragraph one, of the outside and the inside of Lorraine Smart's house? (4)

2 Look at lines 8–18.

Find two phrases that describe Harley's contrasting moods and explain what they tell you about her. (4)

3 Look at lines 12–21.

What do you think are Harley's impressions of Lorraine? Explain your reasons, giving evidence from these lines. (6)

4 Look at lines 22–25.

How does the author create a vivid picture of the backyard? Use quotations from the passage to illustrate your explanations. (4)

5 a) When Harley opens the window she thinks it is 'another planet out here' (line 33). Describe what it is about the view that makes her think this, and explain her consequent thoughts, referring closely to the passage. (5)

b) Why do you think the sky has such an impact on Harley? (2)

Total: 25

3 'Every Good Boy' by David Nicholls

'It's a piano!'

The black lacquered monster loomed in the doorway, my father and Uncle Tony grinning from behind its immense bulk, red-faced from exertion and lunchtime pints. 'They were going to throw it away so I said we'd have it.'

5 My mother looked as if she might cry. 'Take it back, please, I'm begging you.'

'But it's *free*! It's a completely free piano!'

'What are we going to do with a piano, Michael? You can't play it, I can't play it –'

'The kid's going to play it. You're going to learn, aren't you, maestro?'

At the age of nine I was remarkable for being entirely without ability. My sister
10 was a gifted and influential majorette, my older brother could dismantle things, but at that time of my life I could – and this really is no exaggeration – do nothing well. Graceless, charmless, physically and socially inept, I lacked even the traditional intelligence of the nerdy. 'But there must be *something* you can do,' my father would sigh as I fumbled the ball, fell from the tree, bounced clear of the
15 trampoline. 'Everybody can do *something*.'

And what if this piano was the answer? Mozart was composing concertos at nine, and surely the only reason that I hadn't followed suit was because I didn't have access to the same tools. With the piano still on the doorstep, I lifted the lid and pressed a key. It boomed, doomy and industrial, like a sledgehammer striking a
20 girder. I smiled and decided that I would become a prodigy.

The monster was installed in our tiny lounge, looming oppressively over the settee like an angry drunk, smelling of bitter and Benson & Hedges. If a piano isn't good enough for a pub, then it's unlikely to delight the domestic listener, and this really was a terrible machine. The keys were chipped and discoloured
25 like fungal toenails. Someone had written A to G on them in red felt-tip, but pressing middle C caused B and D to sound, too. E and F were interchangeable and the keys beyond this were pure percussion, triangle and bass drum. Even with the lid down, the machine oozed malevolence, thrumming along to the TV as if possessed. Two treacherous candle-holders sprouted from the black lacquer
30 like horns, snagging my mother's cardies and adding to the air of menace. 'I keep thinking there's a corpse in there,' she murmured, glancing over her shoulder as if the piano might hurl itself at her. 'That's why the pedals don't work.'

Level 1

1 Look at lines 2–4.

a) How do the boy's father and Uncle Tony react towards the arrival of the piano?
Write down the words from the passage that tell you this. (2)

Look at line 5.

b) What is the mother's reaction?
Write down the words that tell you this. (2)

2 Look at lines 21–32.

The piano is described as 'a monster' (line 21). Write down, identify and explain two writing techniques that suggest this. (3 + 3)

3 Look at lines 9–15.

a) The narrator feels he is not as good as his brother and sister. Find two quotations and explain what they tell us about his feelings about himself. (4)

b) What does the father think of his son? Write down a short quotation which supports your idea. (2)

4 This text contains humour. In your own words explain what amuses you. (4)

5 'And what if this piano was the answer?' (line 16)

Consider the reactions of the family to the piano and describe what you think might happen next. Base your response on evidence from the passage. (5)

Total: 25

3 'Every Good Boy' by David Nicholls

'It's a piano!'

The black lacquered monster loomed in the doorway, my father and Uncle Tony grinning from behind its immense bulk, red-faced from exertion and lunchtime pints. 'They were going to throw it away so I said we'd have it.'

5 My mother looked as if she might cry. 'Take it back, please, I'm begging you.'

'But it's *free*! It's a completely free piano!'

'What are we going to do with a piano, Michael? You can't play it, I can't play it –'

'The kid's going to play it. You're going to learn, aren't you, maestro?'

At the age of nine I was remarkable for being entirely without ability. My sister
10 was a gifted and influential majorette, my older brother could dismantle things, but at that time of my life I could – and this really is no exaggeration – do nothing well. Graceless, charmless, physically and socially inept, I lacked even the traditional intelligence of the nerdy. 'But there must be *something* you can do,' my father would sigh as I fumbled the ball, fell from the tree, bounced clear of the
15 trampoline. 'Everybody can do *something*.'

And what if this piano was the answer? Mozart was composing concertos at nine, and surely the only reason that I hadn't followed suit was because I didn't have access to the same tools. With the piano still on the doorstep, I lifted the lid and pressed a key. It boomed, doomy and industrial, like a sledgehammer striking a
20 girder. I smiled and decided that I would become a prodigy.

The monster was installed in our tiny lounge, looming oppressively over the settee like an angry drunk, smelling of bitter and Benson & Hedges. If a piano isn't good enough for a pub, then it's unlikely to delight the domestic listener, and this really was a terrible machine. The keys were chipped and discoloured
25 like fungal toenails. Someone had written A to G on them in red felt-tip, but pressing middle C caused B and D to sound, too. E and F were interchangeable and the keys beyond this were pure percussion, triangle and bass drum. Even with the lid down, the machine oozed malevolence, thrumming along to the TV as if possessed. Two treacherous candle-holders sprouted from the black lacquer
30 like horns, snagging my mother's cardies and adding to the air of menace. 'I keep thinking there's a corpse in there,' she murmured, glancing over her shoulder as if the piano might hurl itself at her. 'That's why the pedals don't work.'

Unperturbed, I set to devising soundscapes. Notes to my right I found could be used to suggest falling snowflakes or dropped saucepans, whilst a whole forearm
35 brought down repeatedly on the lower keys conjured up a storm at sea. I worked on compositions – using only the fiercely dissonant black keys, I wrote what I called my 'Chinese Tune'.

There were familiar melodies, too, but the theme to *Jaws* will only enchant for so long, and soon it was decided that I'd need some professional instruction if I were
40 to widen the repertoire and prevent my mother from 'tearing her own ears off'.

The solution lived across the street. Mrs Patricia Chin occupied the handsome semi-detached house opposite us and on summer evenings her piano could be heard through lace-curtained windows – delicate and precise renditions of popular classics, hymns, old Noël Coward numbers above the general clamour
45 of TVs and revving mopeds and bawling. In rare encounters with my mother, she was polite but sour, struggling to conceal her resentment at the new estate on which we lived and which continued to expand into the fields and woodland around what had once been a nice, respectable residential street. Widowed, with a shrinking number of pink-cheeked middle-class pupils at her door, Mrs Chin
50 could not afford to be a snob. She was local, cheap and needy and therefore the ideal teacher for me.

Level 2

1 Look at lines 1–8.

The boy's parents have different reactions to, and feelings about, the arrival of the piano. Using evidence from the text, explain both reactions. (4)

2 Look at lines 21–32.

How does the writer create a vivid picture of the piano? (6)

3 Look at lines 41–51.

What impressions does the writer give us of Mrs Chin? Include quotations in your explanations. (6)

4 The author uses humour to engage the reader. Find two examples of its use and, each time, explain your choice carefully. Use quotations from the passage to illustrate your comments. (4)

5 Do you think the piano and Mrs Chin will be a success? Give reasons for your answer. (5)

Total: 25

4 *The Winning Mind* by Sebastian Coe

Sebastian Coe, who organised the London 2012 Olympics, pays tribute to his father, his coach, whose toughness inspired him to become a double Olympic champion, teaching him that victory can come even from apparent failure.

Just before the 800m final in Prague, I turned to my coach as I left the warm-up track and asked him, 'What do you think I should do today?' He looked at me and said, 'Well, you're not going to win, but if you run as fast and as hard as you can, you'll get on to the rostrum.' And then he added, with a mischievous glint in his
5 eye, 'And we'll find out what the b******s are made of!'

With buckets of adrenaline and his stirring words ringing in my ears, I went off, as the Australians say, 'like free beer'.

I completed the first lap (the halfway stage) faster than anyone had ever done previously in an 800m race. The tactics worked perfectly, until the beginning of
10 the home straight, when the world began to cave in and the adrenaline was replaced by lactic acid.

At this stage, my focus was not on winning a medal; I was concerned simply with reaching the finishing line! Unsurprisingly, Ovett sensed my plight and smoothly eased past, heading for the finishing line. A matter of a few strides later, Olaf
15 Beyer, the East German, powered first past me and then past Ovett to claim a gold medal and a new European record. Ovett won silver and my doggedness gained me bronze.

'Never doubt that for winners, losing hurts.'

The press gave me an absolute slating that day. I was criticised on every side by
20 everybody – apart from my father, who said, 'That was phenomenal! All you have to do next time is to run the second lap as fast as you did the first!' At the end of that race we both knew that I had much hard work to do if I had any hope of winning in the future. My tactics had raised the form of the other runners as well, so we had also learned a whole lot more about the competition. The outcome of
25 that race was the starting point for reshaping my career in the future. It was probably the single most important defining moment in my entire career. We regrouped to consider the outcome and analysed what we had learnt about the competition, as well as assessing what I needed to focus on in order to win in future.

30 Just under a year later, in 1979, I applied the lessons learned in Prague to good effect in Oslo. This time I did run the second lap as fast as the first. Adopting the same tactics, but with the physical and mental skills worked on over the previous year to carry out my intention, I broke the first of my two 800m world records. Records which, in total, stood for eighteen years.

35 Improvement comes from being totally brutal in self-assessment. There was no room for making excuses following my performance in Prague. I knew that if I wanted to beat Ovett, Beyer and others in future, I had to run more miles, improve my strength, refine the track work and increase my conditioning work – and that it had to be done in a more structured way. The same is true in preparing
40 for any role in life.

Level 1

1 Look at the introduction and lines 1–5.

a) Who is Sebastian Coe's coach? (1)

b) What is surprising about the coach's reply, in lines 3–4, to Coe's question? (2)

2 Look at lines 6–7.

a) Identify a metaphor and a simile. (2)

b) In your own words, explain the meaning of these lines. (2)

3 Lines 8–17 describe the race.

Coe starts off feeling joyful but becomes more disappointed as the race progresses.

Find a short quotation that illustrates each stage. Explain your choices. (2 + 4)

4 'It was probably the single most important defining moment in my entire career.' (lines 25–26)

a) In your own words, summarise three lessons learnt by Coe which he took to Oslo in 1979. (3)

b) Reread lines 30–34. What were the two outcomes of those lessons? (2)

5 a) What qualities does Sebastian Coe's father have which make him a good coach? Suggest two and explain your thoughts using ideas from the text. (4)

b) Explain 'Never doubt that for winners, losing hurts' (line 18). (3)

Total: 25

Level 2

4 *The Winning Mind* by Sebastian Coe

Sebastian Coe, who organised the London 2012 Olympics, pays tribute to his father, his coach, whose toughness inspired him to become a double Olympic champion, teaching him that victory can come even from apparent failure.

Just before the 800m final in Prague, I turned to my coach as I left the warm-up trackand asked him, 'What do you think I should do today?' He looked at me and said, 'Well, you're not going to win, but if you run as fast and as hard as you can, you'll get on to the rostrum.' And then he added, with a mischievous glint in his
5 eye, 'And we'll find out what the b******s are made of!'

With buckets of adrenaline and his stirring words ringing in my ears, I went off, as the Australians say 'like free beer'.

I completed the first lap (the halfway stage) faster than anyone had ever done previously in an 800m race. The tactics worked perfectly, until the beginning of
10 the home straight, when the world began to cave in and the adrenaline was replaced by lactic acid.

At this stage, my focus was not on winning a medal; I was concerned simply with reaching the finishing line! Unsurprisingly, Ovett sensed my plight and smoothly eased past, heading for the finishing line. A matter of a few strides later, Olaf
15 Beyer, the East German, powered first past me and then past Ovett to claim a gold medal and a new European record. Ovett won silver and my doggedness gained me bronze.

'Never doubt that for winners, losing hurts.'

The press gave me an absolute slating that day. I was criticised on every side by
20 everybody – apart from my father, who said, 'That was phenomenal! All you have to do next time is to run the second lap as fast as you did the first!' At the end of that race we both knew that I had much hard work to do if I had any hope of winning in the future. My tactics had raised the form of the other runners as well, so we had also learned a whole lot more about the competition. The outcome of
25 that race was the starting point for reshaping my career in the future. It was probably the single most important defining moment in my entire career. We regrouped to consider the outcome and analysed what we had learnt about the competition, as well as assessing what I needed to focus on in order to win in future.

30 Just under a year later, in 1979, I applied the lessons learned in Prague to good effect in Oslo. This time I did run the second lap as fast as the first. Adopting the same tactics, but with the physical and mental skills worked on over the previous year to carry out my intention, I broke the first of my two 800m world records. Records which, in total, stood for eighteen years.

35 Improvement comes from being totally brutal in self-assessment. There was no room for making excuses following my performance in Prague. I knew that if I wanted to beat Ovett, Beyer and others in future, I had to run more miles, improve my strength, refine the track work and increase my conditioning work – and that it had to be done in a more structured way. The same is true in preparing
40 for any role in life.

One more unstructured or haphazard heave would never be enough to enable me to graduate to the next level. The learnings I took from that race provided a signpost for improved performance. They are lessons that I continue to apply:

Never underestimate the competition

45 Do your research and never assume that it is only a two-horse race. While you are focusing on challenging your nearest rival or enjoying your position as market leader, others are working equally hard. Never doubt that there is someone else ready to seize the moment and hungry to displace your market dominance.

Level 2

1 Look at lines 6–7.

Write down and explain two examples of imagery used by the author at the beginning of the race. (4)

2 Look at lines 8–21.

Find and explain three contrasting feelings that Coe experiences. (6)

3 Look at lines 18–34.

a) From lines 18–29, in your own words, summarise three lessons Coe learned which helped his success in Oslo in 1979. (3)

b) What did he achieve in Oslo? (2)

4 Comment on the qualities Sebastian Coe's father has, as his coach. (6)

5 Explain, in your own words, TWO of the following phrases: (4)

- '... to graduate to the next level.' (line 42)
- 'The learnings ... provided a signpost for improved performance.' (lines 42–43)
- '... never assume that it is only a two-horse race.' (line 45)
- 'Never doubt that there is someone else ready to seize the moment and hungry to displace your market dominance.' (lines 47–48)

Total: 25

Level 1

5 *Travels with Charley* by John Steinbeck

The narrator is exploring America with his dog and in this extract he has arrived at Long Island, which hurricane Donna is approaching. *Rocinante* is the name he has given to his truck and his boat is called the *Fayre Eleyne*.

The wind struck on the moment we were told it would, and ripped the water like a black sheet. It hammered like a fist. The whole top of an oak tree crashed down, grazing the cottage where we watched. The next gust stove one of the big windows in. I forced it back and drove wedges in top and bottom with a hand
5 axe. Electric power and telephones went out with the first blast, as we knew they must. And eight-foot tides were predicted. We watched the wind rip at earth and sea like a surging pack of terriers. The trees plunged and bent like grasses, and the whipped water raised a cream of foam. A boat broke loose and tobogganed up on the shore, and then another. Houses built in the benign spring and early summer
10 took waves in their second-storey windows. Our cottage is on a little hill thirty feet above sea level. But the rising tide washed over my high pier. As the wind changed direction I moved *Rocinante* to keep her always to leeward of our big oaks. The *Fayre Eleyne* rode gallantly, swinging like a weathervane away from the changing wind.

15 The boats which had been tethered one to the other had fouled up by now, the tow line under propeller and rudder and the two hulls bashing and scraping together. Another craft had dragged its anchor and gone ashore on a mud bank.

Charley dog has no nerves. Gunfire or thunder, explosions or high winds leave him utterly unconcerned. In the midst of the howling storm, he found a warm
20 place under a table and went to sleep.

The wind stopped as suddenly as it had begun, and although the waves continued out of rhythm they were not wind-tattered, and the tide rose higher and higher. All the piers around our little bay had disappeared under water, and only their piles or handrails showed. The silence was like a rushing sound. The radio told us
25 we were in the eye of Donna, the still and frightening calm in the middle of the revolving storm. I don't know how long the calm lasted. It seemed a long time of waiting. And then the other side struck us, the wind from the opposite direction. The *Fayre Eleyne* swung sweetly around and put the bow into the wind. But the two lashed boats dragged anchor, swarmed down on *Fayre Eleyne*, and bracketed
30 her. She was dragged fighting and protesting downwind and forced against a neighbouring pier, and we could hear her hull crying against the oaken piles. The wind registered over ninety-five miles now.

I found myself running, fighting the wind around the head of the bay towards the pier where the boats were breaking up. I think my wife, for whom the *Fayre*
35 *Eleyne* is named, ran after me, shouting orders for me to stop.

Level 1

1 Look at lines 1–6.

a) Write down two short quotations which describe the impact of the wind. (2)

Look at lines 6–11.

b) In your own words describe two effects on the land because of the force of the hurricane. (2)

2 Look at lines 1–14.

Find an example of a simile, a metaphor and onomatopoeia (a word whose sound echoes its meaning) in these lines. Explain how these help you to have a vivid picture of the hurricane. (2 + 2 + 2)

3 Look at lines 18–20 and 33–35.

a) Write down two short quotations, one about Charley dog and one about the narrator, which show their reactions to the storm. (2)

b) Why do you think they behave as they do? (2)

4 'She was dragged fighting and protesting downwind ... we could hear her hull crying' (lines 30–31).

a) Identify the writing technique used here and describe the picture in your mind. (1 + 2)

b) Why do you think the author chose these emotional words? (2)

5 Hurricane Donna goes through three different stages in this text.

Think of a different adjective to describe each stage. Explain your choices using your own words. (6)

Total: 25

Level 2

5 *Travels with Charley* by John Steinbeck

The narrator is exploring America with his dog and in this extract he has arrived at Long Island, which hurricane Donna is approaching. *Rocinante* is the name he has given to his truck and his boat is called the *Fayre Eleyne*.

The wind struck on the moment we were told it would, and ripped the water like a black sheet. It hammered like a fist. The whole top of an oak tree crashed down, grazing the cottage where we watched. The next gust stove one of the big windows in. I forced it back and drove wedges in top and bottom with a hand
5 axe. Electric power and telephones went out with the first blast, as we knew they must. And eight-foot tides were predicted. We watched the wind rip at earth and sea like a surging pack of terriers. The trees plunged and bent like grasses, and the whipped water raised a cream of foam. A boat broke loose and tobogganed up on the shore, and then another. Houses built in the benign spring and early summer
10 took waves in their second-storey windows. Our cottage is on a little hill thirty feet above sea level. But the rising tide washed over my high pier. As the wind changed direction I moved *Rocinante* to keep her always to leeward of our big oaks. The *Fayre Eleyne* rode gallantly, swinging like a weathervane away from the changing wind.

15 The boats which had been tethered one to the other had fouled up by now, the tow line under propeller and rudder and the two hulls bashing and scraping together. Another craft had dragged its anchor and gone ashore on a mud bank.

Charley dog has no nerves. Gunfire or thunder, explosions or high winds leave him utterly unconcerned. In the midst of the howling storm, he found a warm
20 place under a table and went to sleep.

The wind stopped as suddenly as it had begun, and although the waves continued out of rhythm they were not wind-tattered, and the tide rose higher and higher. All the piers around our little bay had disappeared under water, and only their piles or handrails showed. The silence was like a rushing sound. The radio told us
25 we were in the eye of Donna, the still and frightening calm in the middle of the revolving storm. I don't know how long the calm lasted. It seemed a long time of waiting. And then the other side struck us, the wind from the opposite direction. The *Fayre Eleyne* swung sweetly around and put the bow into the wind. But the two lashed boats dragged anchor, swarmed down on *Fayre Eleyne*, and bracketed
30 her. She was dragged fighting and protesting downwind and forced against a neighbouring pier, and we could hear her hull crying against the oaken piles. The wind registered over ninety-five miles now.

I found myself running, fighting the wind around the head of the bay towards the pier where the boats were breaking up. I think my wife, for whom the *Fayre*
35 *Eleyne* is named, ran after me, shouting orders for me to stop. The floor of the pier was four feet under water, but piles stuck up and offered handholds. I worked my way out little by little up to my breast pockets, the shore-driven wind slapping water in my mouth. My boat cried and whined against the piles, and plunged like a frightened calf. Then I jumped and fumbled my way aboard her. For the first
40 time in my life I had a knife when I needed it. The bracketing wayward boats were pushing *Eleyne* against the pier. I cut anchor line and tow line and kicked them free, and they blew ashore on the mudbank. But *Eleyne's* anchor line was intact, and that great old mud hook was still down, a hundred pounds of iron with spear-shaped flukes wide as a shovel.

Level 2

1 Look at lines 1–14.

How does the writer use imagery to create a vivid impression of the arrival of hurricane Donna? (6)

2 Look at lines 18–20 and 33–35.

Compare Charley dog's and the narrator's reactions to the storm. (4)

3 Look at the vocabulary choices describing the boat in lines 30–39. What do they tell the reader about the narrator's feelings towards his boat? (4)

4 What is the writer's achievement at the end of the passage?

How do you think he feels about his achievement, and how do you think his wife may feel about his actions? (5)

5 Hurricane Donna goes through three different stages in this text, in lines 1–28. Identify a quotation that typifies each stage and explain your choices using your own words. (6)

Total: 25

Level 1

6 *Brazil* by Michael Palin

Michael Palin explores Brazil. He goes to the heart of the rainforest, where human settlement in Brazil began thousands of years ago. He meets a tribe called the Yanomami who up to thirty or forty years ago had had very little contact with the West. They have more contact now but they still live as they have done for thousands of years. The only ways to reach them are by aeroplane or on foot.

The dogs are the first to welcome us. As the pilot, Francisco, eases our plane to a halt at the end of the bumpy grass runway, they race towards us, roused to a frenzy of barking and capering by the sound of the engine and the arrival of an interloper. Behind them figures appear at the doors of the two or three buildings that comprise Demini airstrip. 5

Here in the remote rainforest of north-west Brazil, any arrival from the sky is greeted with expectation. There are no roads that lead here, or even a navigable river. Aeroplanes are the lifeline to the outside world.

At the end of the airstrip are refuelling facilities and a small clinic, staffed by nurses on a monthly roster. There is a kitchen and communications equipment, 10 and some fresh coffee to greet us.

As we unload, figures begin to emerge from a narrow path that leads out of the forest. First come curious little boys in long red shorts, looking, with their black hair, dark eyes and light brown skin, as if they might have stepped straight from the other side of the Pacific, Indonesia or even China. They're followed, a little 15 more warily, by young girls and, with them, older women, most of whom wear nothing but a brief decorated red apron round their waists. The young men, like young men anywhere, make an entrance of self-conscious swagger. They carry bows and very long bamboo arrows with thorn-sharp wooden points. As the women stand and watch from beneath the shady eaves of the clinic, the men 20 gather around appraising us curiously. Sensing I might make a good foil, one of them arches back his bow and sends an arrow flying high into the air. Then he gives me his bow and bids me do the same. Amid much chortling I unleash one of the arrows, which thuds into the ground about five metres away. They seem to like me for having a go and when I take out my notebook they gather around it with 25 great interest. The man with the bow asks for my pen and writes something in my book, in his own language, in fluent longhand. Another likes my straw hat and pops it on his head as unselfconsciously as an MCC member on a hot day at Lord's.

I'm quite relieved by their affability, for my new friends are from the Yanomami 30 tribe and have a history of being fearless and often ferocious fighters. The Yanomami are one of 200 or so indigenous tribes still left from the days when the first Europeans set foot in the country. There were estimated to be some 5 million Indians in Brazil when the Portuguese began to settle here early in the 16th century. Today, after the depredations of slavery, disease and loss of land to 35 loggers, farmers and miners, they number no more than 300,000.

Level 1

1 Look at lines 1–5.

a) The dogs are the first to welcome Michael Palin. In your own words describe the welcome they give him. Give one reason why they arrive on the scene first. (2 + 1)

b) How does the reaction of the people differ from that of the dogs? Why do you think this is? (2)

2 Look at lines 17–24.

a) Write down and explain one short quotation which indicates how the men act when they first meet Palin. (1 + 2)

b) Why do you think the women 'stand and watch from beneath the shady eaves of the clinic' (line 20)? (1)

c) 'Amid much chortling I unleash one of the arrows' (lines 23–24). Explain in your own words what the laughter is about. Why do you think they wanted him to try the bow and arrow? (2 + 1)

3 Look at lines 24–31.

a) Explain in your own words Michael Palin's expectation of the Yanomami tribe in lines 30–31. (2)

b) Describe two things that surprise him in lines 24–29. (4)

4 'Aeroplanes are the lifeline to the outside world.' (line 8)

Name the writing technique used here. Explain, with reference to the whole text, what Michael Palin means here. (3)

5 Michael Palin is a travel writer. He helps the reader to gain an understanding of Brazil using facts and description.

Find a quotation for both facts and description that appeals to you, the reader, and briefly explain why. (4)

Total: 25

6 *Brazil* by Michael Palin

Michael Palin explores Brazil. He goes to the heart of the rainforest, where human settlement in Brazil began thousands of years ago. He meets a tribe called the Yanomami who up to thirty or forty years ago had had very little contact with the West. They have more contact now but they still live as they have done for thousands of years. The only ways to reach them are by aeroplane or on foot.

The dogs are the first to welcome us. As the pilot, Francisco, eases our plane to a halt at the end of the bumpy grass runway, they race towards us, roused to a frenzy of barking and capering by the sound of the engine and the arrival of an interloper. Behind them figures appear at the doors of the two or three buildings
5 that comprise Demini airstrip.

Here in the remote rainforest of north-west Brazil, any arrival from the sky is greeted with expectation. There are no roads that lead here, or even a navigable river. Aeroplanes are the lifeline to the outside world.

At the end of the airstrip are refuelling facilities and a small clinic, staffed by
10 nurses on a monthly roster. There is a kitchen and communications equipment, and some fresh coffee to greet us.

As we unload, figures begin to emerge from a narrow path that leads out of the forest. First come curious little boys in long red shorts, looking, with their black hair, dark eyes and light brown skin, as if they might have stepped straight from
15 the other side of the Pacific, Indonesia or even China. They're followed, a little more warily, by young girls and, with them, older women, most of whom wear nothing but a brief decorated red apron round their waists. The young men, like young men anywhere, make an entrance of self-conscious swagger. They carry bows and very long bamboo arrows with thorn-sharp wooden points. As the
20 women stand and watch from beneath the shady eaves of the clinic, the men gather around appraising us curiously. Sensing I might make a good foil, one of them arches back his bow and sends an arrow flying high into the air. Then he gives me his bow and bids me do the same. Amid much chortling I unleash one of the arrows, which thuds into the ground about five metres away. They seem to like
25 me for having a go and when I take out my notebook they gather around it with great interest. The man with the bow asks for my pen and writes something in my book, in his own language, in fluent longhand. Another likes my straw hat and pops it on his head as unselfconsciously as an MCC member on a hot day at Lord's.

30 I'm quite relieved by their affability, for my new friends are from the Yanomami tribe and have a history of being fearless and often ferocious fighters. The Yanomami are one of 200 or so indigenous tribes still left from the days when the first Europeans set foot in the country. There were estimated to be some 5 million Indians in Brazil when the Portuguese began to settle here early in the
35 16th century. Today, after the depredations of slavery, disease and loss of land to loggers, farmers and miners, they number no more than 300,000.

It's a walk of just over two miles from the clinic to the maloca, the home of this particular group of Yanomami who are to be our hosts for the night. We leave the modern world behind at the end of the airstrip and follow them deep into the
40 forest. A beautiful walk it is too, with sunlight filtering through the foliage and a great quiet, broken only by low voices and the occasional screech of a bird. After 45 minutes the maloca appears abruptly, at the end of the trail. A long circular construction similar in dimension to a small football stadium, which, despite its size, seems to melt into the surrounding forest. Rising protectively behind it is the
45 smooth grey bulk of a granite outcrop, fringed with scrub.

Level 2

1 Look at lines 1–5.

In your own words describe the welcome the dogs give Michael Palin and say why they behave this way. (2)

2 Look at lines 12–24.

a) How do the boys, and the women and the girls, react differently to Palin's arrival? (2)

b) Find two examples of the young men's behaviour towards Michael Palin and explain why you think they behave in this way. (4)

3 Look at lines 22–31.

Explain in your own words Michael Palin's expectation of the Yanomami tribe and explain two things that surprise him about them. (5)

4 Look at lines 37–45.

How does the writer enable the reader to picture the maloca and the journey to it? Use quotations from the end of the passage to illustrate your explanations. (6)

5 Michael Palin, a travel writer, engages the reader by describing:

- the setting
- the people.

Choose an example of each that appeals to you. Explain your choices. (3+3)

Total: 25

Level 1

7 'The Finest Story in the World' by Rudyard Kipling

This is the beginning of a short story which was written in 1891. Charlie Mears works in a bank. He longs to be a writer and seeks the advice of the narrator.

His name was Charlie Mears; he was the only son of his mother who was a widow, and he lived in the north of London, coming into the City every day to work in a bank. He was twenty years old and suffered from aspirations. I met him in a public billiard-saloon where the marker called him by his given name, and he
5 called the marker 'Bulls-eyes.' Charlie explained, a little nervously, that he had only come to the place to look on, and since looking on at games of skill is not a cheap amusement for the young, I suggested that Charlie should go back to his mother.

That was our first step toward better acquaintance. He would call on me sometimes in the evenings instead of running about London with his fellow-
10 clerks; and before long, speaking of himself as a young man must, he told me of his aspirations, which were all literary. [...]

Maybe I encouraged him too much, for, one night, he called on me, his eyes flaming with excitement, and said breathlessly, 'Do you mind – can you let me stay here and write all this evening? I won't interrupt you, I won't really. There's no place for me to write in at my mother's.'

15 'What's the trouble?' I said, knowing well what that trouble was.

'I've a notion in my head that would make the most splendid story that was ever written. Do let me write it out here. It's such a notion!'

There was no resisting the appeal. I set him a table; he hardly thanked me, but plunged into the work at once. For half an hour the pen scratched without
20 stopping. Then Charlie sighed and tugged his hair. The scratching grew slower, there were more erasures, and at last ceased. The finest story in the world would not come forth.

'It looks such awful rot now,' he said, mournfully. 'And yet it seemed so good when I was thinking about it. What's wrong?'

25 I could not dishearten him by saying the truth. So I answered: 'Perhaps you don't feel in the mood for writing.'

'Yes I do – except when I look at this stuff. Ugh!'

'Read me what you've done,' I said. He read, and it was wondrous bad and he paused at all the specially turgid sentences, expecting a little approval; for he was
30 proud of those sentences, as I knew he would be.

'It needs compression,' I suggested, cautiously.

'I hate cutting my things down. I don't think you could alter a word here without spoiling the sense. It reads better aloud than when I was writing it.'

'Charlie, you're suffering from an alarming disease afflicting a numerous class.
35 Put the thing by, and tackle it again in a week.'

'I want to do it at once. What do you think of it?'

'How can I judge from a half-written tale? Tell me the story as it lies in your head.' [...]

I heard him out to the end. It would be folly to allow his idea to remain in his
40 own inept hands, when I could do so much with it. Not all that could be done indeed; but, oh so much!

[1] Tenth

Level 1

1 Look at lines 1–11.

a) Write down four facts that you learn about Charlie from the first paragraph. (2)

b) Reread lines 8–11. How can you tell Charlie looks up to the narrator? Find a quotation and explain your choice. (2)

2 'his eyes flaming with excitement' (lines 12–13)

a) What writing technique is used here? Explain its effect. (1 + 2)

b) Why do you think he is so excited? (1)

3 Look at lines 18–21.

a) Find a phrase from lines 18 and 20 which implies Charlie's enthusiasm. Write it down and explain your choice. (2)

b) Which phrases from lines 20–21 suggest that things are not going well? Find, write down and explain two. (4)

4 Choose and write down one example of dialogue or a thought from each character, the narrator and Charlie, that is typical of them.

Go on to explain what you think it shows about each character. (4)

5 a) At the beginning of the extract, Charlie meets the narrator in the public billiard saloon (lines 1–7). Which character do you sympathise with at this point in the story and why? (2)

b) At the end of the story, do you feel the same? Explain your reasons. (2)

c) Thinking ahead, who do you think will become the hero of the story? Explain your reasons. (3)

Total: 25

7 'The Finest Story in the World' by Rudyard Kipling

This is the beginning of a short story which was written in 1891. Charlie Mears works in a bank. He longs to be a writer and seeks the advice of the narrator.

His name was Charlie Mears; he was the only son of his mother who was a widow, and he lived in the north of London, coming into the City every day to work in a bank. He was twenty years old and suffered from aspirations. I met him in a public billiard-saloon where the marker called him by his given name, and he 5 called the marker 'Bulls-eyes.' Charlie explained, a little nervously, that he had only come to the place to look on, and since looking on at games of skill is not a cheap amusement for the young, I suggested that Charlie should go back to his mother.

That was our first step toward better acquaintance. He would call on me sometimes in the evenings instead of running about London with his fellow-10 clerks; and before long, speaking of himself as a young man must, he told me of his aspirations, which were all literary. […]

Maybe I encouraged him too much, for, one night, he called on me, his eyes flaming with excitement, and said breathlessly, 'Do you mind – can you let me stay here and write all this evening? I won't interrupt you, I won't really. There's no 15 place for me to write in at my mother's.'

'What's the trouble?' I said, knowing well what that trouble was.

'I've a notion in my head that would make the most splendid story that was ever written. Do let me write it out here. It's such a notion!'

There was no resisting the appeal. I set him a table; he hardly thanked me, but 20 plunged into the work at once. For half an hour the pen scratched without stopping. Then Charlie sighed and tugged his hair. The scratching grew slower, there were more erasures, and at last ceased. The finest story in the world would not come forth.

'It looks such awful rot now,' he said, mournfully. 'And yet it seemed so good when I was thinking about it. What's wrong?'

25 I could not dishearten him by saying the truth. So I answered: 'Perhaps you don't feel in the mood for writing.'

'Yes I do – except when I look at this stuff. Ugh!'

'Read me what you've done,' I said. He read, and it was wondrous bad and he paused at all the specially turgid sentences, expecting a little approval; for he was 30 proud of those sentences, as I knew he would be.

'It needs compression,' I suggested, cautiously.

'I hate cutting my things down. I don't think you could alter a word here without spoiling the sense. It reads better aloud than when I was writing it.'

'Charlie, you're suffering from an alarming disease afflicting a numerous class. Put 35 the thing by, and tackle it again in a week.'

'I want to do it at once. What do you think of it?'

'How can I judge from a half-written tale? Tell me the story as it lies in your head.'

Charlie told, and in the telling there was everything that his ignorance had so carefully prevented from escaping into the written word. I looked at him, and 40 wondering whether it were possible, that he did not know the originality, the power of the notion that had come in his way? It was distinctly a Notion among notions. Men had been puffed up with pride by notions not a tithe[1] as excellent and practicable. But Charlie babbled on serenely, interrupting the current of pure fancy with samples of horrible sentences that he purposed to use. I heard him out to the 45 end. It would be folly to allow his idea to remain in his own inept hands, when I could do so much with it. Not all that could be done indeed; but, oh so much!

[1] Tenth

Level 2

1 Look at lines 1–7.

a) Write down four facts that you learn about Charlie in the first paragraph. (2)

b) What do you think 'suffered from aspirations' (line 3) means? What is Charlie's 'aspiration'? (2)

2 'There was no resisting the appeal.' (line 19)

How has the author made Charlie's appeal (lines 17–18) so irresistible and persuasive? (4)

3 Look at lines 12–30.

Describe and explain Charlie's mood changes. (6)

4 Find an example of dialogue or a thought that typifies each character. Explain your choices. (6)

5 Explain your feelings towards each character in your own words. Briefly explain with whom your sympathies lie. (4 + 1)

Total: 25

Level 1

8 *White Fang* by Jack London

Two men, Henry and Bill, are travelling on a sled, pulled by dogs, through a wild, cold landscape. Three of their six dogs have been killed by a wild animal which has been following them.

A few minutes later, Henry, who was now travelling behind the sled, emitted a low, warning whistle. Bill turned and looked, then quietly stopped the dogs. To the rear, from around the last bend and plainly into view, on the very trail they had just covered, trotted a furry, slinking form. Its nose was to the trail, 5 and it trotted with a peculiar, sliding, effortless gait. When they halted, it halted, throwing up its head and regarding them steadily with nostrils that twitched as it caught and studied the scent of them.

'It's the she-wolf,' Bill answered.

The dogs had lain down in the snow, and he walked past them to join his partner 10 in the sled. Together they watched the strange animal that had pursued them for days and that had already accomplished the destruction of half their dog-team.

After a searching scrutiny, the animal trotted forward a few steps. This it repeated several times, till it was a short hundred yards away. It paused, head up, close by a clump of spruce trees, and with sight and scent studied the outfit of the watching 15 men. It looked at them in a strangely wistful way, after the manner of a dog; but in its wistfulness there was none of the dog affection. It was a wistfulness bred of hunger, as cruel as its own fangs, as merciless as the frost itself.

It was large for a wolf, its gaunt frame advertising the lines of an animal that was amongst the largest of its kind.

20 'Stands pretty close to two an' a half feet at the shoulders,' Henry commented. 'An' I bet it ain't far from five feet long.'

'Kind of strange colour for a wolf,' was Bill's criticism. 'I never seen a red wolf before. Looks almost cinnamon to me.'

The animal was certainly not cinnamon-coloured. Its coat was the true wolf-coat. 25 The dominant colour was grey, and yet there was to it a faint reddish hue – a hue that was baffling, that appeared and disappeared, that was more like an illusion of the vision, now grey, distinctly grey, and again giving hints and glints of a vague redness of colour not classifiable in terms of ordinary experience.

'Looks for all the world like a big husky sled-dog,' Bill said. 'I wouldn't be s'prised 30 to see it wag its tail. Hello, you husky!' he called. 'Come here, you, whatever your name is.'

'Ain't a bit scairt of you,' Henry laughed.

Bill waved his hand at it threateningly and shouted loudly; but the animal betrayed no fear. The only change in it that they could notice was an accession 35 of alertness. It still regarded them with the merciless wistfulness of hunger. They were meat, and it was hungry; and it would like to go in and eat them if it dared.

Level 1

1 Look at the introduction and lines 1–7.

a) In the first paragraph Henry notices the wolf. Why do you think Henry gives a 'low, warning whistle' (line 2)? (2)

b) What does Bill do? (1)

c) What are the two men afraid of? Explain your answer in as much detail as possible. (3)

2 Look at lines 3–7.

a) Write down a short quotation that describes the movement of the wolf. What does this suggest about the mood of the wolf? (2)

b) Write down a short quotation that describes the importance of a sense other than sight. Explain it in your own words. (2)

3 Look at lines 16–17.

a) Two similes are used to describe and emphasise the wolf's hunger. Write them both down. (2)

b) Choose one of them and explain in what way it is effective. (2)

4 How would you describe the relationship between the two men? Think of two words or phrases and, each time, explain your thoughts with reference to the text. (4)

5 a) What advantages does the wolf have over Henry and Bill? Suggest three advantages based on the passage. (3)

b) Who do you feel the most sorry for: the wolf, the dogs or Henry and Bill? Explain your reasons. (4)

Total: 25

Level 2

8 *White Fang* by Jack London

Two men, Henry and Bill, are travelling on a sled, pulled by dogs, through a wild, cold landscape. Three of their six dogs have been killed by a wild animal which has been following them.

A few minutes later, Henry, who was now travelling behind the sled, emitted a low, warning whistle. Bill turned and looked, then quietly stopped the dogs. To the rear, from around the last bend and plainly into view, on the very trail they had just covered, trotted a furry, slinking form. Its nose was to the trail, and it trotted with a peculiar, sliding, effortless gait. When they halted, it halted, throwing up its head and regarding them steadily with nostrils that twitched as it caught and studied the scent of them.

'It's the she-wolf,' Bill answered.

The dogs had lain down in the snow, and he walked past them to join his partner in the sled. Together they watched the strange animal that had pursued them for days and that had already accomplished the destruction of half their dog-team.

After a searching scrutiny, the animal trotted forward a few steps. This it repeated several times, till it was a short hundred yards away. It paused, head up, close by a clump of spruce trees, and with sight and scent studied the outfit of the watching men. It looked at them in a strangely wistful way, after the manner of a dog; but in its wistfulness there was none of the dog affection. It was a wistfulness bred of hunger, as cruel as its own fangs, as merciless as the frost itself.

It was large for a wolf, its gaunt frame advertising the lines of an animal that was amongst the largest of its kind.

'Stands pretty close to two an' a half feet at the shoulders,' Henry commented. 'An' I bet it ain't far from five feet long.'

'Kind of strange colour for a wolf,' was Bill's criticism. 'I never seen a red wolf before. Looks almost cinnamon to me.'

The animal was certainly not cinnamon-coloured. Its coat was the true wolf-coat. The dominant colour was grey, and yet there was to it a faint reddish hue – a hue that was baffling, that appeared and disappeared, that was more like an illusion of the vision, now grey, distinctly grey, and again giving hints and glints of a vague redness of colour not classifiable in terms of ordinary experience.

'Looks for all the world like a big husky sled-dog,' Bill said. 'I wouldn't be s'prised to see it wag its tail. Hello, you husky!' he called. 'Come here, you, whatever your name is.'

'Ain't a bit scairt of you,' Henry laughed.

Bill waved his hand at it threateningly and shouted loudly; but the animal betrayed no fear. The only change in it that they could notice was an accession of alertness. It still regarded them with the merciless wistfulness of hunger. They were meat, and it was hungry; and it would like to go in and eat them if it dared.

'Look here, Henry,' Bill said, unconsciously lowering his voice to a whisper because of what he meditated. 'We've got three cartridges. But it's a dead shot. Couldn't miss it. It's got away with three of our dogs, an' we oughter put a stop to it. What d'ye say?'

Henry nodded his consent. Bill cautiously slipped the gun from under the sled-lashing. The gun was on the way to his shoulder, but it never got there, for in that instant the she-wolf leaped sideways from the trail into the clump of spruce trees, and disappeared.

The two men looked at each other. Henry whistled long and comprehendingly.

Level 2

1 In the first paragraph Henry and Bill notice the wolf. Write down their reactions and explain why you think each man reacts in that way. (3)

2 a) Look carefully at the first paragraph.
Write down **two** short quotations which describe the movements of the wolf. Explain how the writer's use of language makes them effective. (4)

b) Look carefully at paragraph four.
Two similes are used to describe the hunger of the wolf as it approaches them. Write them both down and explain the effectiveness of one. (3)

3 What impression do you have of the relationship between the two men? Use evidence to support your ideas. (6)

4 'Henry whistled long and comprehendingly' (line 45). What does this suggest? (2)

5 a) Who do you think – the wolf or the men – is in a stronger position? Explain your answer in detail. (4)

b) For whom do you feel the most sorry: the wolf, the dogs or Henry and Bill? Explain your reasons. (3)

Total: 25

Level 1

9 *Great Expectations* by Charles Dickens

This story was written in 1861. Pip, the narrator of the story, is to meet a runaway prisoner, whom he has met before and who has asked him to get some food. Pip has stolen a pork pie from his kitchen and is on his way to meet the prisoner.

It was a rimy[1] morning, and very damp. I had seen the damp lying on the outside of my little window, as if some goblin had been crying there all night, and using the window for a pocket-handkerchief. Now, I saw the damp lying on the bare hedges and spare grass, like a coarser sort of spiders' webs; hanging itself from 5 twig to twig and blade to blade. On every rail and gate, wet lay clammy, and the marsh mist was so thick, that the wooden finger on the post directing people to our village – a direction which they never accepted, for they never came there – was invisible to me until I was quite close under it. Then, as I looked up at it, while it dripped, it seemed to my oppressed conscience like a phantom devoting 10 me to the Hulks.[2]

The mist was heavier yet when I got out upon the marshes, so that instead of my running at everything, everything seemed to run at me. This was very disagreeable to a guilty mind. The gates and dikes and banks came bursting at me through the mist, as if they cried as plainly as could be, 'A boy with Somebody's 15 else's pork pie! Stop him!' The cattle came upon me with like suddenness, staring out of their eyes, and steaming out of their nostrils, 'Halloa, young thief!' One black ox, with a white cravat on – who even had to my awakened conscience something of a clerical air – fixed me so obstinately with his eyes, and moved his blunt head round in such an accusatory manner as I moved round, that I 20 blubbered out to him, 'I couldn't help it, sir! It wasn't for myself I took it!' Upon which he put down his head, blew a cloud of smoke out of his nose, and vanished with a kick-up of his hind-legs and a flourish of his tail.

However, in the confusion of the mist, I found myself at last too far to the right, and consequently had to try back along the river-side, on the bank of loose stones 25 above the mud and the stakes that staked the tide out. Making my way along here with all despatch, I had just crossed a ditch which I knew to be very near the Battery[3], and had just scrambled up the mound beyond the ditch, when I saw the man sitting before me. His back was towards me, and he had his arms folded, and was nodding forward, heavy with sleep.

30 I thought he would be more glad if I came upon him with his breakfast, in that unexpected manner, so I went forward softly and touched him on the shoulder. He instantly jumped up, and it was not the same man, but another man!

[1] Frosty
[2] Old ships used as prisons
[3] Fortress

Level 1

1 Look at lines 1–8.

a) What is the weather like in this extract? Find and write down two words from the passage that describe it. (2)

b) Find and write down two places affected by the weather. (2)

2 Look at lines 1–10.

a) 'I had seen the damp lying on the outside of my little window, *as if some goblin had been crying there all night*,' (line 2). This is a simile. Find another simile in lines 1–4 and explain what it is describing. (2)

b) Look at lines 5–10. How does Pip know that the marsh mist is thick that morning? Use your own words to explain. (1)

3 a) 'it seemed to my oppressed conscience' (line 9) means that his mind was troubled by something. Suggest two things that you think he is worried about as he sets out that morning. (2)

b) The countryside 'was very disagreeable to a guilty mind' (lines 12–13). From lines 16–22 find two phrases which prove that Pip is feeling guilty. (2)

4 Look at lines 28–32.

a) Pip 'went forward softly' and then 'touched him on the shoulder'. Think of two reasons why he does this. (2)

b) Why does the man quickly jump up? Think of two reasons. (2)

c) Why does Pip not realise it is a different man? (1)

5 a) Pip is thought to be six or seven years old in this part of the story. Think of two words to describe him. Each time explain your choice. (6)

b) Do you feel sorry for Pip or not? Explain your reasons. (3)

Total: 25

Level 2

9 *Great Expectations* by Charles Dickens

This story was written in 1861. Pip, the narrator of the story, is to meet a runaway prisoner, whom he has met before and who has asked him to get some food. Pip has stolen a pork pie from his kitchen and is on his way to meet the prisoner.

It was a rimy[1] morning, and very damp. I had seen the damp lying on the outside of my little window, as if some goblin had been crying there all night, and using the window for a pocket-handkerchief. Now, I saw the damp lying on the bare hedges and spare grass, like a coarser sort of spiders' webs; hanging itself from 5 twig to twig and blade to blade. On every rail and gate, wet lay clammy, and the marsh mist was so thick, that the wooden finger on the post directing people to our village – a direction which they never accepted, for they never came there – was invisible to me until I was quite close under it. Then, as I looked up at it, while it dripped, it seemed to my oppressed conscience like a phantom devoting me to 10 the Hulks.[2]

The mist was heavier yet when I got out upon the marshes, so that instead of my running at everything, everything seemed to run at me. This was very disagreeable to a guilty mind. The gates and dikes and banks came bursting at me through the mist, as if they cried as plainly as could be, 'A boy with Somebody's 15 else's pork pie! Stop him!' The cattle came upon me with like suddenness, staring out of their eyes, and steaming out of their nostrils, 'Halloa, young thief!' One black ox, with a white cravat on – who even had to my awakened conscience something of a clerical air – fixed me so obstinately with his eyes, and moved his blunt head round in such an accusatory manner as I moved round, that I 20 blubbered out to him, 'I couldn't help it, sir! It wasn't for myself I took it!' Upon which he put down his head, blew a cloud of smoke out of his nose, and vanished with a kick-up of his hind-legs and a flourish of his tail.

However, in the confusion of the mist, I found myself at last too far to the right, and consequently had to try back along the river-side, on the bank of loose stones 25 above the mud and the stakes that staked the tide out. Making my way along here with all despatch, I had just crossed a ditch which I knew to be very near the Battery[3], and had just scrambled up the mound beyond the ditch, when I saw the man sitting before me. His back was towards me, and he had his arms folded, and was nodding forward, heavy with sleep.

30 I thought he would be more glad if I came upon him with his breakfast, in that unexpected manner, so I went forward softly and touched him on the shoulder. He instantly jumped up, and it was not the same man, but another man!

And yet this man was dressed in coarse gray, too, and had a great iron on his leg, and was lame, and hoarse, and cold, and was everything that the other man was; 35 except that he had not the same face, and had a flat broad-brimmed low-crowned felt hat on. All this I saw in a moment, for I had only a moment to see it in: he swore an oath at me, made a hit at me – it was a round weak blow that missed me and almost knocked himself down, for it made him stumble – and then he ran into the mist, stumbling twice as he went, and I lost him.

[1] Frosty
[2] Old ships used as prisons
[3] Fortress

Level 2

1 Look at lines 1–8.

a) What is the weather like when Pip wakes that morning? (2)

b) List two places where he notices the results of this weather. (2)

2 Look at lines 1–10.

The author creates a vivid picture of the weather. Find two similes and explain their effectiveness. (4)

3 Look at lines 11–22.

Write down and explain two short quotations that describe Pip's guilt. (4)

4 Look at lines 30–39.

How do you think Pip feels here? Suggest three feelings and explain, with close reference to the text, a reason for each feeling. (6)

5 a) What sort of a boy do you think Pip is?
Explain your thoughts with close reference to the text. (4)

b) In your own words, explain how you feel about Pip in this extract. (3)

Total: 25

Level 1

10 *The History Boys* by Alan Bennett

Set in the early 1980s, the play follows a group of history pupils preparing for university entrance examinations. Mrs Lintott is the boys' usual history teacher and Mr Irwin, a newly hired teacher, has been asked to introduce the boys to a different approach to the subject.

	Mrs Lintott:	Ah, Rudge.
	Rudge:	Miss.
	Mrs Lintott:	How are you all getting on with Mr Irwin?
5	**Rudge**:	It's … interesting, miss, if you know what I mean. It makes me grateful for your lessons.
	Mrs Lintott:	That's nice to hear.
	Rudge:	Firm foundations type thing. Point A. Point B. Point C. Mr Irwin is more … free-range?
	Mrs Lintott:	I hadn't thought of you as a battery chicken, Rudge.
10	**Rudge**:	It's only a metaphor, miss.
	Mrs Lintott:	I'm relieved to hear it.
	Rudge:	You've force-fed us the facts; now we're in the process of running around acquiring flavour.
	Mrs Lintott:	Is that what Mr Irwin says?
15	**Rudge**:	Oh no, miss. The metaphor's mine.
	Mrs Lintott:	Well, you hang on to it.
	Rudge:	Like I'm just going home now to watch some videos of the *Carry On* films[1]. I don't understand why there are none in the school library.
	Mrs Lintott:	Why should there be?
20	**Rudge**:	Mr Irwin said the *Carry Ons* would be good films to talk about.
	Mrs Lintott:	Really? How peculiar. Does he like them, do you think?
	Rudge:	Probably not, miss. You never know with him.
	Mrs Lintott:	I'm now wondering if there's something there that I've missed.
25	**Rudge**:	Mr Irwin says that 'While they have no intrinsic artistic merit (*he is reading from his notes*) – they achieve some of the permanence of art simply by persisting and acquire an incremental significance if only as social history.'
	Mrs Lintott:	Jolly good.
30	**Rudge**:	'If George Orwell[2] had lived, nothing is more certain than that he would have written an essay on the *Carry On* films.'
	Mrs Lintott:	I thought it was Mr Hector who was the Orwell fan.
	Rudge:	He is. Mr Irwin says that if Orwell were alive today he'd be in the National Front.
	Mrs Lintott:	Dear me. What fun you must all have.
35	**Rudge**:	It's cutting-edge, miss. It really is.

Timms:	Where do you live, sir?
Irwin:	Somewhere on the outskirts, why?
Timms:	'Somewhere on the outskirts,' oooh. It's not a loft, is it, sir?

	Akthar:	Do you exist on an unhealthy diet of takeway food, sir, or do you
40		whisk up gourmet meals for one?
	Timms:	Or is it a lonely pizza, sir?
	Irwin:	I manage. No questions from you, Dakin?
	Dakin:	What they want to know, sir, is, 'Do you have a life? Or are we it? Are we your life?'

[1] A series of comedy films which gently mocked British institutions and customs
[2] An English novelist and journalist who wrote extensively on social injustice

Level 1

1 Look at line 3.

Why do you think Mrs Lintott stops Rudge to ask this question? (3)

2 Look at lines 7–13.

Rudge suggests the two teachers, Mrs Lintott and Mr Irwin, have different teaching styles: Mrs Lintott treats them like 'battery chickens' and Mr Irwin is 'free-range'.

Explain, using short quotations from lines 12–13, what this tells you about their teaching styles. (4)

3 What are your impressions of Mrs Lintott?

Use short quotations or your own ideas, based on the text, to support your answer. (6)

4 Look at lines 1–35.

Rudge is teasing and mocking in his conversation with Mrs Lintott. Find three short quotations which show this, and explain your choices. (6)

5 Look at lines 36–45.

a) Why do you think the boys ask Mr Irwin so many questions? (1)

b) What is the key question? (1)

c) How will Mr Irwin's response to this question affect the boys' opinion of him? (4)

Total: 25

Level 2

10 *The History Boys* by Alan Bennett

Set in the early 1980s, the play follows a group of history pupils preparing for university entrance examinations. Mrs Lintott is the boys' usual history teacher and Mr Irwin, a newly hired teacher, has been asked to introduce the boys to a different approach to the subject.

	Mrs Lintott:	Ah, Rudge.
	Rudge:	Miss.
	Mrs Lintott:	How are you all getting on with Mr Irwin?
5	**Rudge**:	It's … interesting, miss, if you know what I mean. It makes me grateful for your lessons.
	Mrs Lintott:	That's nice to hear.
	Rudge:	Firm foundations type thing. Point A. Point B. Point C. Mr Irwin is more … free-range?
	Mrs Lintott:	I hadn't thought of you as a battery chicken, Rudge.
10	**Rudge**:	It's only a metaphor, miss.
	Mrs Lintott:	I'm relieved to hear it.
	Rudge:	You've force-fed us the facts; now we're in the process of running around acquiring flavour.
	Mrs Lintott:	Is that what Mr Irwin says?
15	**Rudge**:	Oh no, miss. The metaphor's mine.
	Mrs Lintott:	Well, you hang on to it.
	Rudge:	Like I'm just going home now to watch some videos of the *Carry On* films[1]. I don't understand why there are none in the school library.
	Mrs Lintott:	Why should there be?
20	**Rudge**:	Mr Irwin said the *Carry Ons* would be good films to talk about.
	Mrs Lintott:	Really? How peculiar. Does he like them, do you think?
	Rudge:	Probably not, miss. You never know with him.
	Mrs Lintott:	I'm now wondering if there's something there that I've missed.
25	**Rudge**:	Mr Irwin says that 'While they have no intrinsic artistic merit (*he is reading from his notes*) – they achieve some of the permanence of art simply by persisting and acquire an incremental significance if only as social history.'
	Mrs Lintott:	Jolly good.
30	**Rudge**:	'If George Orwell[2] had lived, nothing is more certain than that he would have written an essay on the *Carry On* films.'
	Mrs Lintott:	I thought it was Mr Hector who was the Orwell fan.
	Rudge:	He is. Mr Irwin says that if Orwell were alive today he'd be in the National Front.
	Mrs Lintott:	Dear me. What fun you must all have.
35	**Rudge**:	It's cutting-edge, miss. It really is.

Timms:	Where do you live, sir?
Irwin:	Somewhere on the outskirts, why?
Timms:	'Somewhere on the outskirts,' oooh. It's not a loft, is it, sir?

	Akthar:	Do you exist on an unhealthy diet of takeway food, sir, or do you
40		whisk up gourmet meals for one?
	Timms:	Or is it a lonely pizza, sir?
	Irwin:	I manage. No questions from you, Dakin?
	Dakin:	What they want to know, sir, is, 'Do you have a life? Or are we it? Are we your life?'
45	**Irwin**:	Pretty dismal if you are. Because (*giving out books*) these are as dreary as ever.
		If you want to learn about Stalin, study Henry VIII.
		If you want to learn about Mrs Thatcher, study Henry VIII.
		If you want to know about Hollywood, study Henry VIII.
50		The wrong end of the stick is the right one. A question has a front door and a back door. Go in the back, or better still, the side.
		Flee the crowd. Follow Orwell. Be perverse.
		And since I mention Orwell, take Stalin. Generally agreed to be a monster, and rightly. So dissent. Find something, anything, to say in
55		his defence.
		History nowadays is not a matter of conviction.
		It's a performance. It's entertainment. And if it isn't, make it so.
	Rudge:	I get it. It's an angle. You want us to find an angle.

[1] A series of comedy films which gently mocked British institutions and customs
[2] An English novelist and journalist who wrote extensively on social injustice

Level 2

1 Look at lines 7–13.

Rudge suggests the two teachers, Mrs Lintott and Mr Irwin, have different teaching styles. Identify the metaphors used to describe each and explain what this tells you about them. (4)

2 What impressions do you have of Mrs Lintott? (4)

3 Look closely at how Rudge speaks to Mrs Lintott.

What does this tell you about his character and intentions? Use quotations to support your thoughts. (6)

4 Look at lines 36–47.

a) In what ways will Mr Irwin's response to the question 'Are we your life?' (line 44) affect the relationship between him and the boys? (4)

b) What do Mr Irwin's actual response and behaviour indicate? (3)

5 Look at lines 49–57.

Find and explain two quotations which demonstrate how Mr Irwin wants the boys to approach their work. (4)

Total: 25

Paper 2 Section A: Reading – Poetry

→ Introduction

The poems and questions in this poetry section of the book are designed to test understanding as well as powers of analysis and evaluation. Poets from different eras have been selected and range from Samuel Taylor Coleridge to Phoebe Hesketh. The subject matter or message of the poem therefore reflects the historical context and the issues of their time. This enables practice in the understanding of a range of vocabulary, the way the words are put together, the form and the structure.

Look back to page 1, the Introduction to Paper 1 Section A: Reading – Literary prose for guidance on reading and answering questions. Note, however, that there are a few additional requirements specific to poetry. Poems may need more than one reading in order to absorb their message, rhythm, rhyme, and 'feel'. Question types are similar to those on the literary prose reading paper, but have a particular emphasis on poetic techniques, where relevant. An insightful understanding of the poem's message and structure is also required, which may include reference to rhythm, rhyme and metre.

The accompanying answer book provides additional advice for the teacher and parent but also enables candidates to understand the final expectation and so monitor their progress.

Levels 1 & 2

1 'Paint Box' by Phoebe Hesketh

He tried to tell them what he felt,
could say it only in colours …
Sunday's white paper shading to grey
of evening clocks and bells-in-the-rain.
5 Monday morning, bright yellow brass
of a cock crowing.
Story-time, purple.
Scarlet is shouting in the playground.

His world's a cocoon
10 round as an egg, an acorn
sprouting green.
The schoolroom square and hard,
his desk hard and square
facing the enemy blackboard.

15 'You must learn to read,' they said
and gave him a painting-book alphabet.
Apple swelled beautifully red. Balloon
expanded in blue.

C was a cage for a bird;
20 his brush wavered through
painting himself
a small brown smudge inside.

Level 1

1 Write down two short quotations which suggest that the poem is set in a school some years ago. (2)

2 Look at lines 1–8.

Choose three colours referred to in stanza one. Using short quotations, which include a colour, explain what each of these tell you about the boy. (6)

3 Look at lines 9–14.

a) 'His world's a cocoon/round as an egg' (lines 9–10).

Identify the two poetic techniques used here and explain one of them. (2 + 1)

b) Personification is giving objects human characteristics. Find an example of personification in stanza two. What does this tell you about the boy? (2)

4 Pick out the repeated words in stanza two. Why do you think the poet has written these lines like this? (2)

5 a) Look at lines 15–18.

The boy feels content as he starts to paint. Find a quotation that shows this and explain your choice. (3)

b) Look at lines 19–22.

Here the boy feels unhappy. Find a quotation that shows this and explain your choice. (3)

6 For what reasons do you think the poet chose the title 'Paint Box'? (4)

Total: 25

Level 2

1 Look at the opening stanza.

Explain the significance of three of the colours in stanza one. (6)

2 Look at stanza two.

The poet creates a vivid impression of the boy's life in stanza two.

Identify and explain three ways in which the poet achieves this. You should refer to the techniques used. (6)

3 Look at lines 15–18.

How does the boy feel as he begins to paint? (3)

4 Explain, in detail, what you think is suggested by the last four lines of the poem. (6)

5 For what reasons do you think the poet chose the title 'Paint Box'? (4)

Total: 25

2 'Fox' by Ted Hughes

Who
Wears the smartest evening dress in England?
Checks his watch by the stars
And hurries, white-scarfed,
5 To the opera
In the flea-ridden hen-house
Where he will conduct the orchestra?

Who
With a Robin Hood mask over his eyes
10 Meets King Pheasant the Magnificent
And with silent laughter
Shakes all the gold out of his robes
Then carries him bodily home
Over his shoulder,
15 A swag-bag?

And who
Flinging back his Dracula cloak
And letting one fang wink in the moonlight
Lifts off his top hat
20 Shows us the moon through the bottom of it
Then brings out of it, in a flourish of feathers,
The gander we locked up at sunset?

Level 1

1 a) Find and write down two short quotations which suggest when the fox hunts. (2)

b) Which three creatures does the fox hunt, according to this poem? (3)

2 Ted Hughes dresses up the fox in each stanza to be a different person.

a) In the first stanza he describes the fox as an orchestra conductor. Write down two short quotations which suggest this. (2)

b) In the second stanza why do you think the poet gives the fox 'a Robin Hood mask over his eyes' (line 9)? (2)

c) In the third stanza, find and explain one way in which the fox is likened to a magician. (2)

3 Explain the metaphors as they are used in this passage: (4)

- 'opera' (line 5) in stanza one
- 'gold' (line 12) in stanza two

4 What impression do you have of the fox's character in each stanza?

Write down a short quotation from each stanza and explain your choice each time. (6)

5 Do you think this fox is to be admired, or not? Consider the whole poem including the ending. (4)

Total: 25

Level 2

1 When does the fox go hunting and for what? (2)

2 What identity does the poet give the fox in each stanza? Find and explain a phrase which supports your choice each time. (6)

3 What different feelings does the fox exhibit in each stanza? (6)

4 How do the following devices add to the poem's effect?

- repetition
- questions
- imagery

Identify examples and explain your choices. (6)

5 Do you think Ted Hughes' fox is to be admired, or not? Consider the whole poem including the ending. (5)

Total: 25

3 'Frustration' by Tom Earley

The pigeons sunbathed on the autumn lawn,
Collecting warmth against the coming cold.
Today their curious posture puzzled me:
Instead of their accustomed nestling down,
5 Squeezed in the grass as though they covered eggs,
They stood erect and still, facing one way
Heads held high on rigid necks.

Remaining quiet, I looked around
And saw behind the birds, alarmingly close,
10 A hunting cat poised for the kill.
His black body was pressed into the green
As flat as a plate. With ears held down
And head lowered, he watched.
His mouth mimed inaudible cries.

15 He eased himself forward like a snake.
Now he was a yard from the nearest bird.
I held my breath. I did not see him spring,
Only heard the explosion of wings
And saw the massed flight: no hostage
20 Left, no victim. Like a swift scythe
The cat's angry tail slashed the turf.

Level 1

1 Look at stanza one.

'Today their curious posture puzzled me' (line 3).

Explain in your own words why the poet is puzzled about how the pigeons are behaving. (4)

2 Reread the description of the hunting cat in lines 11–15.

a) Write down a simile from these lines and describe the image it creates in your head. (2)

b) 'His mouth mimed inaudible cries.' (line 14)

Name a poetic technique used here and explain the picture you see. (1 + 2)

3 a) Look at lines 17–20. What do you notice about the sentence lengths? How and why do you think the poet has written the sentences like this? (2 + 2)

b) Find an example of repetition in lines 18–20. Why does the poet use repetition here? (2)

4 Look at the title of the poem. Find and explain two short quotations, from the final stanza, which support the poet's choice of title. (4)

5 a) Find and explain one line from stanza two that indicates what the poet thought might be the outcome. (4)

b) The poet does nothing. Explain one possible reason for this. (2)

Total: 25

Level 2

1 Look at stanza one.

Why is the poet puzzled about the pigeons' behaviour?
Explain in your own words. (4)

2 Look at lines 11–15.

What poetic techniques does the poet use to enable us to picture the hunting cat? What effect do you think each creates? (6)

3 Lines 17–20 provide a vivid account of the moment of crisis.
Comment on three writing devices the poet uses to achieve this. (6)

4 a) What did the poet think might be the outcome of the story within the poem? Find and briefly explain three quotations from stanza two that support this. (3)

b) Explain the choice of title with particular reference to the final stanza. (2)

5 Comment on the mood created in the first and last sentences of the poem and consider how effective they are as an opening and ending. (4)

Total: 25

4 'Flag' by John Agard

What's that fluttering in a breeze?
It's just a piece of cloth
that brings a nation to its knees.

What's that unfurling from a pole?
5 It's just a piece of cloth
that makes the guts of men grow bold.

What's that rising over a tent?
It's just a piece of cloth
that dares the coward to relent.

10 What's that flying across a field?
It's just a piece of cloth
that will outlive the blood you bleed.

How can I possess such a cloth?
Just ask for a flag my friend.
15 Then bind your conscience to the end.

Level 1

1 Look at the structure of the poem.

a) There is a conversation in it. What pattern do you notice about this conversation in the first four stanzas? (2)

b) Find two examples of repetition in the first four stanzas. (2)

2 The poet uses personification in the last line of the first four stanzas to describe the effects of the flag. Explain your understanding of:

- 'that makes the guts of men grow bold.' (line 6) (2)
- 'that dares the coward to relent.' (line 9) (2)
- 'that will outlive the blood you bleed.' (line 12) (2)

3 a) Write down the words that describe the movement of the flag in the first lines of stanzas two, three and four. In your own words explain their meaning. (3)

b) Describe the scene that is suggested in each of those stanzas. (3)

4 a) Give reasons why you think the speaker, in the last stanza, wants to possess a flag. (3)

b) Look at the last line. What do you think are the difficulties in having a flag? (2)

5 How far do you agree or disagree that a flag is just a piece of cloth? (4)

Total: 25

Level 2

1 Look at the form of the poem.

a) What patterns does the poet create in stanzas one to four? Identify four. (4)

b) How does the format change in the final stanza? (2)

2 Identify the poetic technique used in the last line of stanzas two, three and four and explain your understanding of each line. (4)

3 Look at stanzas two, three and four.

a) Write down the words that describe the movement of the flag in the first lines of stanzas two, three and four. In your own words explain their meaning. (3)

b) Describe the scene that is suggested in each of those stanzas. (3)

4 Look at the final stanza.

a) Why do you think the speaker wants to possess a flag? (1)

b) What is your interpretation of the last line of the poem? (2)

5 To what extent do you agree or disagree that a flag is 'just a piece of cloth'? (6)

Total: 25

5 'The Caged Bird in Springtime' by James Kirkup

What can it be
This curious anxiety?
It is as if I wanted
To fly away from here.

5 But how absurd!
I have never flown in my life,
And I do not know
What flying means, though I have heard,
Of course, something about it.

10 Why do I peck the wires of this little cage?
It is the only nest I have ever known.
But I want to build my own,
High in the secret branches of the air.

I cannot quite remember how
15 It is done, but I know
That what I want to do
Cannot be done here.

I have all I need –
Seed and water, air and light.
20 Why, then, do I weep with anguish,
And beat my head and my wings
Against these sharp wires, while the children
Smile at each other, saying: 'Hark how he sings'?

Level 1

1 Why do you think the poem starts with a question? Suggest two reasons. (2)

2 Look at lines 1–17.

Instinct is driving the bird to do two things which it is unable to do. What are they? Write down two quotations that tell you this. (4)

3 a) 'Why, then, do I weep with anguish,
And beat my head and my wings
Against these sharp wires,' (lines 20–22)
What is the bird's mood? Write down and explain a brief quotation from these lines to support your thoughts. (3)

b) '... while the children/Smile at each other, saying: "Hark how he sings"?' (lines 22–23)
What is the children's mood? Write down and explain a quotation from these lines to support your thought. (3)

4 Using ideas of your own and from the text, explain the advantages for the bird within the cage. Go on to explain any disadvantages that might come with its freedom. (6)

5 a) Think about the message of the poem. Suggest two points the poet is making. (4)

b) How far do you agree with the poet? (3)

Total: 25

Level 2

1 The bird is 'Caged' in 'Springtime' and suffers a 'curious anxiety' (line 2). Explain two reasons for its anxiety. Why do you think it feels like this? (4)

2 Comment on the 'question and answer' structure used throughout the poem. How does this help your understanding of the bird? (2 + 2)

3 Look carefully at the language of the last four lines of the poem and comment, in as much detail as you can, on the poet's vocabulary choices that describe the bird's and the children's behaviour. (6)

4 a) 'High in the secret branches of the air.' (line 13)
Identify the poetic technique used here and explain what you think the poet is trying to achieve. (3)

b) The poem is expressed in a relatively simple way.
Why do you think the poet chose to write it in this way? (3)

5 In your own words sum up the message the poet is giving to the reader. Do you agree with the poet? (5)

Total: 25

6 'Going for Water' by Robert Frost

The well was dry beside the door,
And so we went with pail and can
Across the fields behind the house
To seek the brook if still it ran;

5 Not loth to have excuse to go,
Because the autumn eve was fair
(Though chill), because the fields were ours,
And by the brook our woods were there.

We ran as if to meet the moon
10 That slowly dawned behind the trees,
The barren boughs without the leaves,
Without the birds, without the breeze.

But once within the wood, we paused
Like gnomes that hid us from the moon,
15 Ready to run to hiding new
With laughter when she found us soon.

Each laid on other a staying hand
To listen ere we dared to look,
And in the hush we joined to make
20 We heard, we knew we heard the brook.

A note as from a single place,
A slender tinkling fall that made
Now drops that floated on the pool
Like pearls, and now a silver blade.

Level 1

1 Look at lines 1–4.

Write down and explain two quotations which show that the weather had been dry. (4)

2 Look at lines 5–8.

a) The children are keen to go for water. Find a quotation that suggests this. (2)

b) Explain in your own words two different reasons why they feel this. (2)

3 Write down a short quotation, from stanzas three and four and five, to show how the children's mood is eager, then joyful and finally cautious as they go for water. Explain your choices. (3 + 3)

4 Look at lines 21–24.

a) Robert Frost uses onomatopoeia to describe the sound of the brook. Write down the example and explain why you think he chose this word. (2)

b) 'Now drops that floated on the pool/Like pearls' (lines 23–24).

Which poetic technique has the poet used here? (1)

c) '... and now a silver blade.' (line 24)

Which poetic technique has the poet used here? Explain the picture you see. (1 + 2)

5 Look at the poem as a whole.

a) Reread the last word on each line and explain the rhyme pattern the poet creates. (2)

b) What do you notice about the rhythm of the poem? (2)

c) How do the rhyme and the rhythm affect the pace at which you read the poem? (1)

Total: 25

Level 2

1 Look at stanza two.

Explain how you think the children are feeling in stanza two. (4)

2 Look at stanza three.

How does the poet emphasise the season for the reader? Use short quotations to illustrate your analysis. (6)

3 Look at stanza five.

Explain how this stanza can be seen as a turning point in the poem. (5)

4 The poet creates a vivid impression of the brook in the last stanza. Identify and explain three ways in which the poet achieves this. You should refer to the techniques used and the effects each creates. (6)

5 How do the rhyme scheme and rhythm help to make the poem effective? Explain your answer fully. (4)

Total: 25

7 'The Hermit' by W.H. Davies

What moves that lonely man is not the boom
Of waves that break against the cliff so strong;
Nor roar of thunder, when that travelling voice
Is caught by rocks that carry far along.

5 'Tis not the groan of oak tree in its prime,
When lightning strikes its solid heart to dust;
Nor frozen pond when, melted by the sun,
It suddenly doth break its sparkling crust.

What moves that man is when the blind bat taps
10 His window when he sits alone at night;
Or when the small bird sounds like some great beast
Among the dead, dry leaves so frail and light.

Or when the moths on his night-pillow beat
Such heavy blows he fears they'll break his bones;
15 Or when a mouse inside the papered walls,
Comes like a tiger crunching through the stones.

Level 1

1 The poet writes about what does and does not make an impression on the lonely man.

a) Stanzas one and two describe what does **not** make an impression on the man. List one thing from stanza one and one thing from stanza two. (2)

b) But in stanzas three and four, things **do** make an impression on him. Again list one thing from each stanza. (2)

c) What do you notice about the things that move him and make an impression on him and the things that do not? (3)

2 Davies enables us to 'hear' the sounds the lonely man hears by using onomatopoeia (words that imitate the sound they describe). Select two examples from the whole poem, write them down and explain what you 'hear'. (4)

3 a) 'like some great beast' (line 11) is a simile. Why is the bird described in this way? (1)

b) Find a simile in the last stanza, write it down and explain its effect on the reader. (3)

4 a) What do you notice about the rhyme scheme? (1)

b) The poem also has a regular rhythm. In what ways do you think the regularity of the rhyme and rhythm fit the topic of the poem? (3)

5 The man in the poem is a hermit, which is a person who lives alone.

a) What clues, apart from the title, are there to suggest that he is a loner? (2)

b) Do you think he is happy being alone? (2)

c) Think of one reason why you would like his lifestyle and one reason why not. (2)

Total: 25

Level 2

1 a) List four sights and sounds that do not make an impression on the man. (2)

b) List four sounds that do make an impression on him. (2)

c) What do you find surprising about the things that move him and those that do not? (2)

2 How does the author use sound devices to make his poem vivid? Select two examples and explain their effectiveness. (4)

3 Identify the two similes used in stanzas three and four. Write them down and, for each, explain its effectiveness. (4)

4 Look carefully at the rhythm and rhyme within the poem.

What do you notice about each? Explain the combined effect of both on the reader. (4 + 2)

5 a) Having read this poem, what do you think a hermit is? (1)

b) Do you think the man is happy? Give your reasons why or why not. (4)

Total: 25

8 'Sleet' by Norman MacCaig

The first snow was sleet. It swished heavily
Out of a cloud black enough to hold snow.
It was fine in the wind, but couldn't bear to touch
Anything solid. It died a pauper's death.

5 Now snow – it grins like a maniac in the moon.
It puts a glove on your face. It stops gaps.
It catches your eye and your breath. It settles down
Ponderously crushing trees with its airy ounces.

But today it was sleet, dissolving spiders on cheekbones,
10 Being melted spit on the glass, smudging the mind
That humped itself by the fire, turning away
From the ill wind, the sky filthily weeping.

Level 1

1 a) Name the weather condition described in each stanza. (1)

b) Choose and write down a verb or verb phrase from each stanza that you think is effective in describing each weather condition. Explain your choices. (6)

2 a) 'It died a pauper's death.' (line 4)

This describes the sleet as it lands. Which poetic technique is used here? (1)

b) Find an example of a simile from stanza two. (1)

c) '... dissolving spiders on cheekbones' (line 9).

What is the name given to this technique? Explain the picture it creates in your mind. (1 + 2)

3 a) What do you notice about both the sentences and punctuation in stanzas one and two? What effect do these have on the rhythm of the poem in those stanzas? (4)

b) What do you notice about the sentence length in the last stanza? What effect does this have on the rhythm of the poem here? (2)

4 a) Name the tense used in each stanza. (1)

b) Can you think of a reason why the poet uses tenses in this way? (2)

5 In the final stanza the poet describes how the sleet makes some people feel.

'... smudging the mind

That humped itself by the fire, turning away

From the ill wind, the sky filthily weeping.' (lines 10–12)

Explain in your own words what the poet means in these lines. (4)

Total: 25

Level 2

1 a) Look at stanzas one and two. What are the main differences between the sleet and the snow in stanzas one and two? Find quotations to explain and support your ideas. (6)

b) Look at stanza three. Summarise, in your own words, the reactions of people to the sleet in the final stanza. (3)

2 Look at the words used in the last line of each stanza. Identify and explain the use of poetic techniques. (6)

3 Identify the use of tenses in each stanza. Give one reason why you think the poet chose to write the poem like this. (2)

4 Comment on the sentence lengths in stanzas two and three. What is the effect of these on the rhythm of those stanzas? (4)

5 Give two supported reasons why you think the poet chose to give the poem the title 'Sleet', commenting on his attitudes and feelings. (4)

Total: 25

Levels 1 & 2

9 Extract from 'The Rime of the Ancient Mariner' by Samuel Taylor Coleridge

A ship is driven off course and eventually reaches Antarctica, where an albatross[1] appears.

The ship drove fast, loud roared the blast,
And southward aye we fled.

And now there came both mist and snow,
And it grew wondrous cold:
5 And ice, mast-high, came floating by,
As green as emerald.

And through the drifts the snowy clifts
Did send a dismal sheen:
Nor shapes of men nor beast we ken[2] –
10 The ice was all between.

The ice was here, the ice was there,
The ice was all around:
It cracked and growled, and roared and howled,
Like noises in a swound[3]!

15 At length did cross an Albatross,
Through the fog it came;
As it had been a Christian soul,
We hailed it in God's name.

It ate the food it ne'er had eat,
20 And round and round it flew.
The ice did split with a thunder-fit;
The helmsman steered us through!

And a good south wind sprung up behind;
The Albatross did follow,
25 And every day, for food or play,
Came to the mariner's hollo[4]!

In mist or cloud, on mast or shroud,
It perched for vespers[5] nine;
Whiles all the night, through fog-smoke white,
30 Glimmered the white moonshine.

[1] A huge sea-bird
[2] Saw and recognised
[3] The act of fainting
[4] Loud cry
[5] Evening prayers

Level 1

1 a) Look at lines 1–14. Summarise briefly what they are about. (2)

b) Look at lines 15–30. Summarise briefly what they are about. (2)

2 a) The sailors are feeling worried in the first 14 lines. Explain why you think this is. Support your reason with two short quotations. (3)

b) The sailors are feeling relieved in lines 15–30. Explain why you think this is. Support your reason with two short quotations. (3)

3 Look at lines 11–14 which describe the ice.

a) Write down the two lines which indicate that they are surrounded by ice. What do you notice and why do you think the poet wrote the lines like this? (3)

b) The poet uses sound effects to describe the sounds of the ice. Write down two examples of this. In what way are these words effective? (2 + 1)

4 This is an extract from a ballad: a poem which tells a story. Every stanza is regular and follows the same pattern of rhythm and rhyme.

a) What do you notice about the pattern of rhythm **or** rhyme? (2)

b) How does the pattern make the poem, and the story it is telling, more vivid? (2)

5 'At length did cross an Albatross' (line 15).

a) Who do the sailors think sent it? Write down two ways in which it helps their journey. (1 + 2)

b) What do you think the albatross might be a symbol of? What message do you think Coleridge, in 1798, was trying to give his readers? (1 + 1)

Total: 25

Level 2

1 a) Summarise briefly what the first 14 lines are about. (1)

b) Summarise briefly what lines 15–30 are about. (1)

2 The sailors experience various different emotions during the part of the voyage described in the passage. With close reference to the text, explain what you think these might be. (6)

3 Look at lines 5–14.

How does the author make the description of the ice vivid? Refer closely to the text in your answer. (6)

4 This is an extract from a ballad: a poem which tells a story.

What do you notice about the pattern of the rhythm and the rhyme? How do they both make the poem, and the story it is telling, effective and engaging? (6)

5 'At length did cross an Albatross' (line 15).

a) The albatross becomes a symbol for the sailors. What happens to make the sailors think the albatross is a symbol? What does it symbolise to them? (2 + 2)

b) In this section of the poem, what message do you think Coleridge, in 1798, was conveying? (1)

Total: 25

10 'Silence' by Thomas Hood

There is a silence where hath been no sound,
There is a silence where no sound may be,
In the cold grave – under the deep, deep sea,
Or in wide desert where no life is found,
5 Which hath been mute, and still must sleep profound;
No voice is hush'd – no life treads silently,
But clouds and cloudy shadows wander free,
That never spoke, over the idle ground:
But in green ruins, in the desolate walls
10 Of antique palaces, where Man hath been,
Though the dun fox or wild hyaena calls,
And owls, that flit continually between,
Shriek to the echo, and the low winds moan –
There the true Silence is, self-conscious and alone.

Level 1

1 Look at lines 1–2.

In your own words, explain the two types of silence referred to here. (2)

2 a) Look at lines 1–8. Write down three short quotations which explain where silence is to be found. (3)

b) Look at lines 9–14. Write down two short quotations which explain 'where Man hath been' (line 10). (2)

3 Repetition is used in lines 3–6. Identify two examples of repetition and explain the effect of one of them. (4)

4 Onomatopoeia is the use of words to create sounds. Write down two examples of onomatopoeia used to describe nature in lines 11–13. Explain the effects they have on the reader. (2 + 4)

5 a) Look at the last word in lines 9–12. What do you notice about the rhyme pattern created? (1)

b) Look at the last word in lines 13–14. What do you notice about the rhyme pattern and why do you think the poet wrote the lines like this? (1 + 2)

6 'There the true Silence is, self-conscious and alone.' (line 14)

The poet feels the 'true' silence is 'where Man hath been'. Explain why the poet thinks the only real silence is where man has been. (4)

Total: 25

Level 2

1 a) In your own words, explain what the poet means by 'silence' in the first two lines. (2)

b) From lines 3–4, identify three places where the poet thinks there is a silence and explain how these contrast with the silent places referred to in lines 9–10. (4)

2 Look at lines 1–6.

Find two different examples of repetition and explain the effect of each. (4)

3 Look at lines 9–13.

What atmosphere has the poet created? How is this sustained? (6)

4 The regular rhyme scheme changes in this poem. Where do the changes come and what do the changes signify? (5)

5 What do you understand by the last line of the poem? (4)

Total: 25

Paper 1 Section B: Writing task

Introduction

The titles in this writing task section of the book, which are common to both Level 1 and Level 2 candidates, are designed to test writing for a practical purpose and writing on a literary topic. In the exam, candidates make a choice and select one title. Questions 1–3 offer a selection of titles to write for a practical purpose and question 4 offers a choice of two titles on literary topic writing. To aid practice in this book, the literary topic titles have been separated out from the practical purpose titles. The practice this book provides per task is therefore as follows:

Writing for a practical purpose

- Page 61 – genres explained: to argue, persuade, explain, advise and inform
- Pages 61–62 – examples of questions laid out in exam format to give the candidate practice in making the best choice
- Pages 63–65 – additional questions, grouped according to genre for further practice

Writing for a practical purpose should demonstrate an awareness of the purpose of the task, display features of the chosen genre and be appropriate in content, tone and style.

Writing on a literary topic

- Pages 62–63 – examples of questions laid out in exam format to give the candidate practice in making the best choice

Writing on a literary topic should demonstrate insight, knowledge and understanding of books. The ability to unpick a question, and then select and transfer only the relevant information and examples, is an important skill.

Using the practice questions

Although the plan may not be passed on to the senior school, careful planning will ensure that compositions display a clear progression of ideas and are well structured, containing sufficient detail. Ideas should be clearly expressed and provide a wide and suitable vocabulary. Spelling, grammar and syntax should be correct, and work should be presented neatly.

These pages may be used as exam practice under timed conditions, in which case approximately 35 minutes should be allowed for choosing, planning and writing one essay. It is advisable to leave time to check at the end. The titles could also be used to practise writing skills without the time pressure.

The accompanying answer book has further guidance on writing for a practical purpose and writing on a literary topic, and shows and explains the ISEB marks and descriptors.

➜ Writing for a practical purpose – genres

Questions/titles fall into five genres: to argue, persuade, explain, advise and inform.

Argue

The purpose is to present objectively two balanced sides to a topic. An opinion may be required in the conclusion.

This could be in the form of a letter, article or essay.

Persuade

The purpose is to persuade the reader to adopt the writer's point of view.

This could be in the form of a letter, article, essay or speech.

Explain

The purpose is to explain to the reader what, how and/or why something has been done.

This could be in the form of a letter, article, essay, speech, diary or leaflet.

Advise

The purpose is to advise the reader what they should do, how they should do it and why.

This could be in the form of a letter, article, essay, speech or leaflet.

Inform

The purpose is to pull together relevant information, such as opinions, facts, viewpoints and statements, to inform the reader. Within this genre candidates may be asked to write about themselves or from their own experience.

This could be in the form of a letter, article, essay, speech, diary or leaflet.

➜ Writing for a practical purpose – questions 1–3

SECTION B: WRITING TASK

Write on any ONE of the following topics. Each is worth 25 marks.

Credit will be given for good spelling, punctuation and presentation as well as for the appropriate use of language for the task.

A1 Is it better to travel or to arrive?

Write an essay in which you consider both points of view.

A2 Has there been an occasion when you have experienced two different emotions within a short space of time?

Write a detailed account of such a time.

A3 Write a speech, to be presented to your debating society, in which you attempt to persuade your audience that:

'Choice, in whatever you do, is a wonderful thing.'

B1 Write a letter to the local community, as if you are the Chief of Police, explaining that there has been a sighting of a 'big cat' or beast in the area.

Within your letter you may like to include:

- information about the recent sightings
- what the beast looks like
- safety advice to the general public
- advice about what to do if you spot the beast.

B2 Is it ever permissible to do wrong?

Write a balanced argument which considers both sides of this question.

B3 Town or country living?

Do you think it is better to live in the town or the countryside?

Write from your point of view, explaining carefully, which you prefer and why.

C1 Write an article for your school magazine entitled 'How to survive exams'.

C2 Write a review for a new technological product which informs consumers of its merits and drawbacks.

C3 What role does luck play in people's lives? Write an essay explaining your views.

D1 Write a discursive essay which considers the question: 'Cars, a blessing or a curse?'

D2 Explain what you have learnt about yourself and others through playing sport.

D3 If you had the power to do so, what changes would you make to schools in Britain today? Write a letter to the Minister for Education outlining your ideas and suggestions.

→ Writing on a literary topic – question 4

SECTION B: WRITING TASK

Write on any ONE of the following topics. Each is worth 25 marks.

Credit will be given for good spelling, punctuation and presentation as well as for the appropriate use of language for the task.

E1 EITHER

a) 'We read to know we are not alone.' (C.S. Lewis)

Describe a book you have read where you have become caught up and identified with the main characters and their experiences.

OR

b) We can empathise with characters in a text when they meet moments of crisis which can change the course of events.

By referring to your own reading, describe how the crisis affected the characters. In your enjoyment of the book how important was this turning point?

E2 EITHER

a) Do we have to sympathise with, approve of and like key characters in books to be able to enjoy the story? Discuss with reference to one or more books and their characters.

OR

b) Is there a book which you did not enjoy at the outset, but then enjoyed immensely by the end? In your answer explain what it was that made you change your mind.

E3 EITHER

a) 'Never judge a book by its movie' (J.W. Eagan). Discuss this statement.

OR

b) What makes a good central character in a novel? With reference to one or more books you have read, outline the qualities needed to engage the reader.

E4 EITHER

a) Have you read a book which is set in the past, the future or an unfamiliar environment? Compare its setting to the world that you know today. How far did the different setting enhance or detract from your enjoyment of the book?

OR

b) Choose a book which you feel has an unforgettable ending. Explain the reasons for your choice.

E5 EITHER

a) Can reading a novel affect or change your mood? If so, how and why?

OR

b) 'There is more treasure in books than in all the pirate's loot on *Treasure Island*' (Walt Disney). What kinds of 'treasure' do you look for in your reading? In your essay refer to one or more books you have read.

E6 EITHER

a) Is there a book which has made you think differently about your own life, and which you would recommend to your own children in years to come? Explain your choice referring in detail to this book.

OR

b) Choose a book where loyalty has been a key theme. Using episodes from the book explain the importance of loyalty.

➜ Writing for a practical purpose – additional practice questions

The following provide writing practice in the various genres.

Argue

1. Is it ever right to fight?
2. Is exploration worthwhile or a waste of money? Discuss.
3. Do you consider money to be the root of all evil or a necessary evil?
4. People who get into difficulties while taking part in outdoor activities or dangerous sports have only themselves to blame; other people should not risk their lives to help them. Discuss.
5. Is it always right to keep a secret? Write a balanced argument.
6. Television talent shows encourage young people to aspire to fame and fortune.

   Write a magazine article in which you set out your views on this topic.

Persuade

7 School trips: educational or a waste of time? Write a letter to a headmasters' forum where you strongly present your own view.

8 Is cheating in tests out of control? Yes or no?

9 Write a speech for your debating society where you support or refute the statement: 'Good health is only the responsibility of the individual.'

10 Write a persuasive essay about the benefits of listening to and/or playing music.

11 Media or meetings? Facebook or face to face? Write a speech in which your aim is to persuade your listeners to take your point of view.

12 Think of a position of responsibility in your school that you would like to hold.

Write a letter of application to your head teacher in which you attempt to persuade them that you are the best pupil for the job.

You may like to think about:

- head boy/girl
- prefect
- sports captain
- school council
- or any other position of your choice.

Explain

13 Write a speech, to deliver to your school assembly, on the important qualities of friendship.

14 What would you like to be or do when you leave school? Write an article, called *A Day in the Life of* ... from the point of view of an imaginary character who has a job in which you are interested.

15 There are a wide range of pressures on teenagers today. Explain what you think are the main pressures and how they affect you and your friends.

16 Is there an object which is very precious to you and your family? Explain its significance to all members of your family.

17 All experiences teach us something. Explain how far this is true in your own life.

18 A French student is coming to stay with your family and will attend your school for a week.

Write an informal letter to them in which you explain what life will be like in your family or at your school.

Advise

19 Write a letter to your head teacher in which you advise him or her of your ideas about how to spend time between Common Entrance and the end of the summer term.

20 Write about a time when you were lost. Within your writing provide some advice for others in a similar situation.

21 How to survive school. Give your advice.

22 Write an article on safety, for someone your age, who is going to take up your favourite sport or hobby.

23 How can you happily spend time alone? Write a piece for a teenage magazine where you provide some suggestions and advice, based on your own experience.

Inform

24 Write an essay which outlines and informs how animals can be helpful to man.

25 Describe a time when things did not work out as you expected.

26 Write about a time when you had to move house.

27 Write an article about a person you admire, from history or the present day.

28 You have been asked to produce an information leaflet for a historical tourist attraction. Choose and write about an attraction that you have visited.

29 You have just taken an exam and received the result.

Write two diary entries to describe:

- the day of the exam
- the day you received the result.

Paper 2 Section B: Writing task

Introduction

The questions/titles in this writing task section of the book, which are common to both Level 1 and Level 2 candidates, are designed to test creative writing.

- Page 66 – genres explained: imaginative, descriptive and narrative
- Pages 67–68 – examples of questions laid out in exam format to give the candidate practice in making the best choice
- Pages 69–70 – additional questions, grouped according to genre for further practice

Although the plan may not be passed on to the senior school, careful planning will ensure that essays are well structured and relevant to the task. Writing should demonstrate originality, flair and creativity and be engaging in content, tone and style, with a lively and interesting use of vocabulary. Spelling, grammar and syntax should be correct, and work should be presented neatly.

These pages may be used as exam practice under timed conditions, in which case approximately 35 minutes should be allowed for choosing, planning and writing one essay. It is advisable to leave time to check at the end. The titles could also be used to practise writing skills without time pressure.

The accompanying answer book has further guidance on creative writing, and shows and explains the ISEB marks and descriptors.

Writing to provoke imaginative, descriptive and narrative responses – genres

Imaginative

Writing to provoke imaginative, descriptive and narrative responses requires creative thinking. Imaginative writing, in the context of this exam, falls into the descriptive or narrative genre.

Descriptive

Realistic: the writing will describe a person, place or object so that the reader can clearly visualise, and enter into, the writer's experience.

Imaginative: the writing will describe images and sensations, not necessarily bound by realism, and may evoke or invent other worlds.

Narrative

Realistic: the writing will tell a story or part of a story based on believable events, characters and settings.

Imaginative: the writing will tell a story or part of a story not necessarily based on the candidate's own experience or bound by realism.

The writing will be prompted by a title, quotation, proverb or sentence.

➜ Writing to provoke imaginative, descriptive and narrative responses – questions

SECTION B: WRITING TASK

Write on any ONE of the following topics. Each is worth 25 marks.

Credit will be given for good spelling, punctuation and presentation as well as for imaginative and exciting use of vocabulary.

A1 'Goodbye,' I whispered. I knew I would never return again.

Write a story which includes these lines.

A2 Write a story or descriptive essay using one of the following titles:

a) Solitude

b) The Stranger

c) Voices

A3 'First come, first served.'

Write about this in any imaginative way you wish.

A4 The Best Things in Life are Free.

Use this title to write a description or a story.

B1 Write a story which includes the words: 'It was the bitter smell of despair.'

B2 Write a description of someone who is considered to be eccentric.

B3 Write about one of the following:

a) Almost Midnight

b) Thin Ice

c) A Twist in the Tale

B4 Write about a journey, real or imagined, where the weather made a significant impact on your progress.

C1 Write a story using one of the following titles:

a) The Last Train

b) The Cage

c) On My Own

C2 'When I was but thirteen or so

I went into a golden land,' (Katharine Tynan)

Describe the golden land you entered.

C3 Write about a real or imaginary experience where the senses, other than sight, were very important.

C4 An Unexpected Outcome

D1 Write a short story or descriptive piece using the following title: The House on the Corner of the Street.

D2 Write a story which begins or ends with this sentence: 'We were friends, but on that day we were strangers.'

D3 Choose one of the following titles to write a story or descriptive piece:

a) Underwater

b) Underground

c) Under a Cloud

D4 Describe a frightening incident or confrontation that you either witnessed or were involved in and explain, in your writing, how you felt afterwards.

E1 The Night has a Thousand Eyes

E2 Write about a time when you were taken by surprise or you surprised someone.

E3 Write a story using one of the following titles:

a) The Box

b) Breaking the Rules

c) Case Closed

E4 How I see the world in 2050

F1 'What is this life if, full of care,

We have no time to stand and stare.' (W.H. Davies)

Write about the things worth staring at.

F2 The door was ajar, I couldn't resist it ...

F3 Write a description of a chase from the hunter's and/or the prey's point of view.

F4 Write a short story or descriptive piece using one of the following:

a) Breaking the Code

b) We Knew we Shouldn't be There

c) Stormy Waters

G1 Write two contrasting descriptions of your school, one at lunchtime and one in the evening after dark.

G2 Write a story which includes this line:

'The wind buffeted me, knocking me nearly senseless.'

G3 Write a story or descriptive piece of writing using one of the following titles:

a) The Hiding Place

b) The Meeting

c) The Pathway

G4 Write a story which includes a torch, a piece of string and a key.

➜ Writing to provoke imaginative, descriptive and narrative responses – additional practice questions

The following questions provide writing practice in the various genres.

Imaginative

Imaginative responses, in the context of this exam, fall into the descriptive or narrative genre. The titles and prompts in this section may be used in either way.

1 'I like nonsense, it wakes up the brain cells. Fantasy is a necessary ingredient in living.' (Dr Seuss) Use this quotation to write a story or descriptive essay of your choice.

2 The Glass Cupboard

3 Every Picture Tells a Story

4 A Golden Key Can Open Any Door

5 Write a descriptive piece, either real or imagined on: my idea of heaven or my nightmare surroundings.

6 The Turning Point

7 Bank Holiday Boredom

8 Insomnia

9 Out of the Box

10 'I laid me down upon the shore

And dreamed a little space;

I heard the great waves break and roar;

The sun was on my face.' (Frances Cornford)

Use these lines as the inspiration for a piece of writing of your own.

Descriptive

11 Describe as vividly as you can the place which has most affected your life.

12 The Fisherman's Friend

13 'Slowly, silently, now the moon

Walks the night in her silver shoon;' (Walter de la Mare)

Use this extract as a basis for a descriptive essay.

14 First Thing in the Morning

15 Describe a creature which has made an impression on you.

16 A room can say a great deal about the person who owns it.
Describe a room that you think does this.

17 Mr Hardcastle

18 Describe a dangerous place you know and explain what makes it dangerous.

19 Storm at Sea

20 Describe a place you are familiar with at two different times of day or times of year.

Narrative

21 'And then there was silence.' Include this sentence within your story.

22 The Decision

23 Write about a time when you felt restricted or restrained.

24 The Wrong Side of Town

25 One Way Only

26 Release!

27 'A fool and his money are soon parted.' Use this proverb as a stimulus for a story.

28 'A dog is a man's best friend.' Write a story based on this sentence.

29 But the letter arrived too late ...

30 Write a story which ends with an apology.

31 Walls Have Ears

32 'Tomorrow is another day,' my father said as he turned out the light.

Use this as the final sentence in a story.

33 A Case of Mistaken Identity

34 'Two's company and three's a crowd.'
Include this sentence in a story of your choice.

35 Write a story that involves two characters, a dog and a river.

36 Disappointment

37 The Trick

38 Continue this story in any way you wish:

'Opening the front door, she stopped dead in her tracks.'

39 The Secret Passage

40 Entering the Danger Zone